NICKY EPSTEIN
Knit a Square
Create a Cuddly Creature

NICKY EPSTEIN
Knit a Square
Create a Cuddly Creature

FROM FLAT TO FABULOUS • **A Step-by-Step Guide**

Nicky Epstein Books

AN IMPRINT OF
SIXTH&SPRING BOOKS
NEW YORK

Nicky Epstein Books

An Imprint of Sixth&Spring Books
161 Avenue of the Americas, New York, NY 10013
sixthandspring.com

Executive Editor
CARLA SCOTT

Editorial Assistant
JACOB SEIFERT

Yarn Editor
MATTHEW SCHRANK

Technical Illustrations
LORETTA DACHMAN

Photography
JACK DEUTSCH

Background Illustrations
KEELY BRANDON

**Vice President/
Editorial Director**
TRISHA MALCOLM

Publisher
CAROLINE KILMER

Creative Director
JOE VIOR

Production Manager
DAVID JOINNIDES

President
ART JOINNIDES

Chairman
JAY STEIN

Library of Congress Cataloging-in-Publication Data

Names: Epstein, Nicky, author.
Title: Knit a square, create a cuddly creature: from flat to fabulous – a step-
by-step guide / by Nicky Epstein.
Description: First edition. | New York : Sixth&Spring Books, [2016] Includes
index.
Identifiers: LCCN 2016003247 | ISBN 9781942021667 (pbk.)
Subjects: LCSH: Soft toy making–Patterns. | Stuffed animals (Toys)
Classification: LCC TT174.3 .E67 2016 | DDC 745.592--dc23
LC record available at http://lccn.loc.gov/2016003247

Dedication

This book is dedicated to all those whose kindness to, compassion for, and love of all animals show a goodness of character and heart—people like Christine Farrow, Jo Brandon, and Diana Book. And especially to my father, Ben Quinones, who taught me to respect all animals with whom we share this earth. And to my husband Howard, who is a loveable animal himself!

Nicky Epstein

Table of Contents

Introduction

Knit a Square, Create a Cuddly Creature was inspired by an experimental idea of mine to make an animal using just one knitted square. The few animals I had done were so exciting and fun to make that I decided to fill an entire book with them.

Each project starts with one square that is then sewn, stuffed, and shaped to form the animal. Legs, ears, tails, or other simple embellishments may be added to bring the critters to life.

While not entirely new, this simple construction concept was underdeveloped and more or less unknown to the general knitting public. So, my publishing team and I worked very hard to create clear charts, diagrams, and easy-to-follow instructions. After you get the basics down, I think you will be as fascinated with all the varieties of construction as I am—and you'll be very proud of yourself.

With just one square, you can create gifts for all your little (and big) loved ones. Please experiment with different yarns (unless otherwise noted), colors, and even stitch patterns. For extra fun, make animals in different sizes—as tiny or as huge as you'd like—simply by using different yarn weights (see sheep on page 11).

If you have any unused knit squares around the house, go ahead and use them for a special bunny or cat. Added embellishments can also make your animal extra special and personal.

Happy Animal Knitting!

Nicky

Here are a few extra ideas:
• Hide a music box inside to make a musical toy.
• Make an animal pillow.
• Use wool and then felt your animal (see page 59).
• Make a series of small animal ornaments to decorate a tree, wreath, or door hanger.
• Weight the bottom and use as a doorstop.

HERE ARE A FEW GENERAL TIPS FOR MAKING YOUR BLOCK ANIMALS:

• Most of the animals use only one skein of yarn. When working intarsia color blocks, cut long lengths of each color needed or make butterfly bobbins (see page 143) and always use a separate bobbin for each block of color.

• Markers are placed onto the square to indicate the various sections. You can use locking stitch markers, small safety pins, or small lengths of scrap yarn.

• Running stitches are sewn onto the knitted square to outline the areas that need to be gathered. Use the working yarn to sew these stitches and always leave long ends that will be later used for gathering. Some of the swatches shown in the instructions show the running stitches. For clarity only, we used a contrasting-color yarn.

• It is helpful to pin together the larger sections before seaming for a neat and even seam. For the legs in particular, you are usually seaming stitches to rows and one side may be longer than the other. Be sure to ease the longer edge into the shorter edge.

• Always leave long tails from the cast on and bound off stitches. These ends may be used for seaming.

• When finished with all seaming, secure and hide each end by tying a knot close to the animal and then weaving it through the body.

• Stuffing is a key element to making these animals. It is best to use polyester stuffing which is available at most craft stores. Start with a small amount, shaping the piece as you go. If instructed to stuff firmly, continue to add stuffing until firm, but do not stuff so much that the stitches pull apart and show the stuffing. When stuffing small areas, such as the tips of the legs or shaping the body and head joints, use a blunt tapestry needle to push up the stuffing.

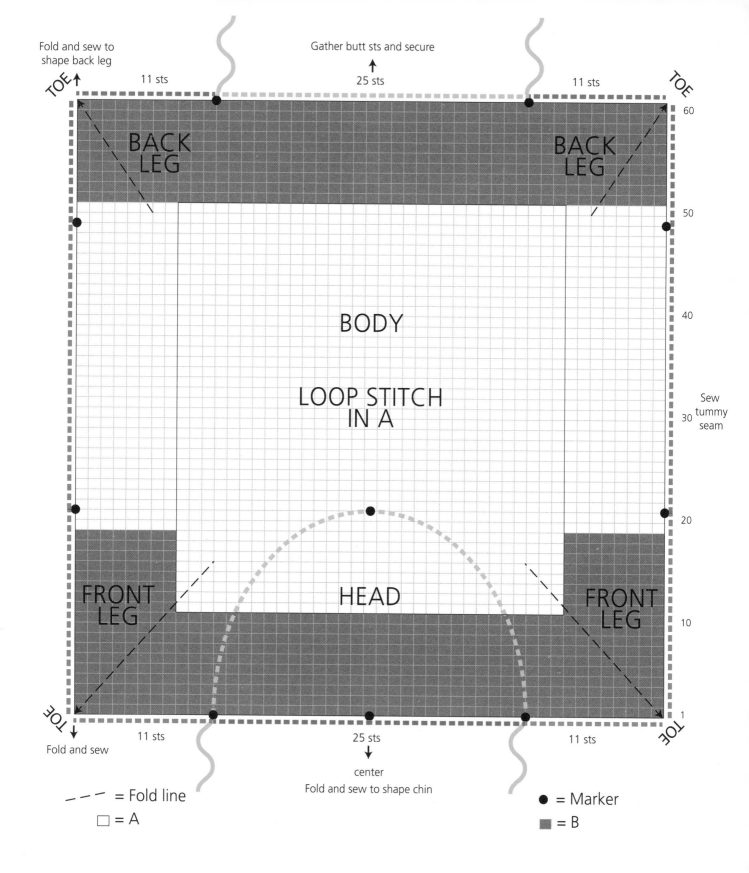

Fold and sew to shape back leg

Gather butt sts and secure

TOE

11 sts

25 sts

11 sts

TOE

60

BACK LEG

BACK LEG

50

BODY

LOOP STITCH IN A

40

Sew tummy seam

30

20

FRONT LEG

HEAD

FRONT LEG

10

TOE

11 sts

25 sts

11 sts

TOE

1

Fold and sew

center
Fold and sew to shape chin

- - - = Fold line

□ = A

● = Marker

▨ = B

12

Sally and her herd
are a knitter's best friends.
Their lovely coats allow
us to spin, dye, and knit
beautiful things.

Materials

Note Seven different yarns weights are used. Each square is knit with the same number of sts and rows; the different yarn weights determine the size of the square, and therefore the finished sheep.

- 1¾oz/50g balls (each approx 273yd/250m) of Cascade 220 Fingering (wool) in #8505 White (A) and #8555 Black (B) **1**
- One pair size 3 (3.25mm) needles, OR SIZE TO OBTAIN GAUGE
- 1 1¾oz/50g balls (each approx 133.5yd/125m) of Cascade 220 Superwash Sport (wool) **3** in #871 White (A) and #815 Black (B)
- One pair size 6 (4mm) needles, OR SIZE TO OBTAIN GAUGE
- 1 3½oz/100g balls (each approx 220yd/200m) of Cascade 220 Superwash Worsted (wool) in #871 White (A) and #815 Black (B) **4**
- One pair size 7 (4.5mm) needles, OR SIZE TO OBTAIN GAUGE
- 1 3½oz/100g balls (each approx 150yd/137.5m) of Cascade 220 Superwash Aran (wool) in #871 White (A) and #815 Black (B) **4**
- One pair size 9 (5.5mm) needles, OR SIZE TO OBTAIN GAUGE
- 1 3½oz/100g balls (each approx 128yd/117m) of Cascade 128 Superwash (wool) in #871 White (A) and #815 Black (B) **5**
- One pair size 10 (6mm) needles, OR SIZE TO OBTAIN GAUGE
- 1 8.82oz/250g balls (each approx 123yd/112.5m) of Cascade Magnum (wool) in #8505 White (A) and #0050 Black (B) **6**
- One pair size 17 (12.75mm) needles, OR SIZE TO OBTAIN GAUGE

- 1 40oz/1,134g skeins (each approx 125yd/113m) of Bagsmith Merino Yarn Bumps (wool/nylon) in Pearl (A) and Onyx (B) **7**
- One pair size 35 (19mm) needles, OR SIZE TO OBTAIN GAUGE

For all versions
- Small amount of pink yarn in corresponding yarn weight for face embroidery
- 2 beads in corresponding size for eyes
- Bells (optional)
- Stitch markers and tapestry needle
- Polyester stuffing

Gauges

- 28 sts and 36 rows to 4"/10cm over St st using size 3 (3.25mm) needles and Cascade 220 Fingering.
- 22 sts and 28 rows to 4"/10cm over St st using size 6 (4mm) needles and 220 Superwash Sport
- 20 sts and 26 rows to 4"/10cm over St st using size 7 (4.5mm) needles and 220 Superwash Worsted
- 16 sts and 20 rows to 4"/10cm over St st using size 9 (5.5mm) needles and 220 Superwash Aran
- 14 sts and 21 rows to 4"/10cm over St st using size 10 (6mm) needles and 128 Superwash
- 8 sts and 12 rows to 4"/10cm over St st using size 15 (10mm) needles and Magnum
- 4 sts and 5 rows to 4"/10cm over St st using size 35 (19mm) needles and Merino Yarn Bumps

TAKE TIME TO CHECK GAUGE.

Stitch Glossary

LS (Loop Stitch) Worked on wrong side. Insert RH needle into st as if to knit it. Wind yarn over RH needle and around index finger of left hand 3 times, then over RH needle point once more. Draw all loops through st on LH needle, then slip loops to LH needle. Insert RH needle through back of these loops and original st and knit them together through back loops.

Note

When working chart, use separate lengths (butterflies) of yarn for each block of color and when changing colors, twist yarns on WS to prevent holes in work.

Square

With B, using desired yarn and needles, cast on 47 sts. Beg with a knit row, work in St st (k on RS, p on WS) for 10 rows.
Row 11 (RS) With B k8, with A k31, with B k8.
Row 12 With B p8, with A k1, *LS, k1; rep from * to last 8 sts, with B p8.
Note For sheep made with Merino Yarn Bumps, center 31 A sts are worked in rev St st (p on RS, k on WS) instead of loop st.
Row 13 Rep row 1.
Row 14 With B p8, with A k2, *LS, k1; rep from * to last A st, k1, with B p8.
Rep rows 1–4 rows once more. Break yarns. Join A and work rows 1–4 of as before but with A only, 8 times, then work rows 1 and 2 once more. Break yarn.
With B and beg with a k row, work 10 rows in St st. Bind off.

Tail

With A, cast on 7 sts. Work in St st for 6 rows (for sheep in Magnum, work 10 rows).
Row 1 (RS) K2, SK2P, k2.
Row 2 P5.
Row 3 K1, SK2P, k1.
Row 4 P3.
Row 5 SK2P.
Secure last st.

Ears

With B, cast on 5 sts. Work in St st for 6 rows.
Row 1 (RS) K1, SK2P, k1.
Row 2 P3.
Row 3 SK2P. Secure last st.

Assembly

Lay square on a flat surface. Mark center 25 sts along cast-on edge. Mark center st and measure up 20 rows from center st and place another marker. Cut a piece of color A approx 25"/63.5cm long and sew running sts to outline head, foll diagram for placement and leaving a long length at both ends. Mark center 25 sts along bound-off edge. Cut a piece of color A approx 15"/38cm long and sew running sts along these sts for the butt. Place markers each side at 20 rows from cast-on to mark front legs and 12 rows from bound-off edges to mark back legs.

Here's How

1

Running stitches are sewn to outline the head and butt. A contrasting-color yarn is used here for clarity.

2

Pull the two long ends left over from the running stitches and gather the fabric to form the head.

3

When the outer edges meet, tie the ends together tightly into a double knot. Stuff the head firmly.

4

Fold the cast-on stitches of the head in half and sew the edges together to form the chin.

5

Fold the sides of the leg so that the edges meet, easing the longer side to the shorter side if necessary, and pin in place.

6

Gather the butt stitches by pulling on the ends from the running stitches and tie the ends together in a double knot. Then sew the leg seams.

Head
Pull both ends of the running-st yarn that marked the head, gathering the fabric until the outer edges meet at the center, then tie the ends in a double knot tightly. Stuff the head firmly. Fold head in half and sew cast-on sts tog for chin seam.

Front Legs
Fold one front leg so that side edges meet (blue dotted lines) and form a point at the outer edge (toe), easing the longer edge into the shorter edge and pin the edges together. Sew the side edges together.

Fold and sew the other front leg in same way. Stuff the legs firmly.

Butt
Pull both ends of the yarn that marked the butt, gathering the fabric, then tie the ends in a double knot.
Be sure that the yarn is pulled tightly.

Back Legs
Fold one back leg so that side edges meet (green dotted lines) and form a point at the outer edge and pin the edges together. Sew the side edges together.

Fold and sew the other back leg in same way. Stuff the legs firmly.

Tummy
Stuff the remainder of the body firmly. Pin the remaining two sides together and with A, sew the tummy seam.

Finishing Details
With A make a duplicate st for eyes. Sew bead to center. With pink yarn, embroider nose and mouth. Sew ears to head, leaving approx 2"/5cm between the ears. Sew tail to top of butt. ❀

7

Using the tail end if possible, sew the two sides of the leg together.

8

After stuffing the body firmly, sew the remaining two sides together for the belly seam, shown here using mattress stitch.

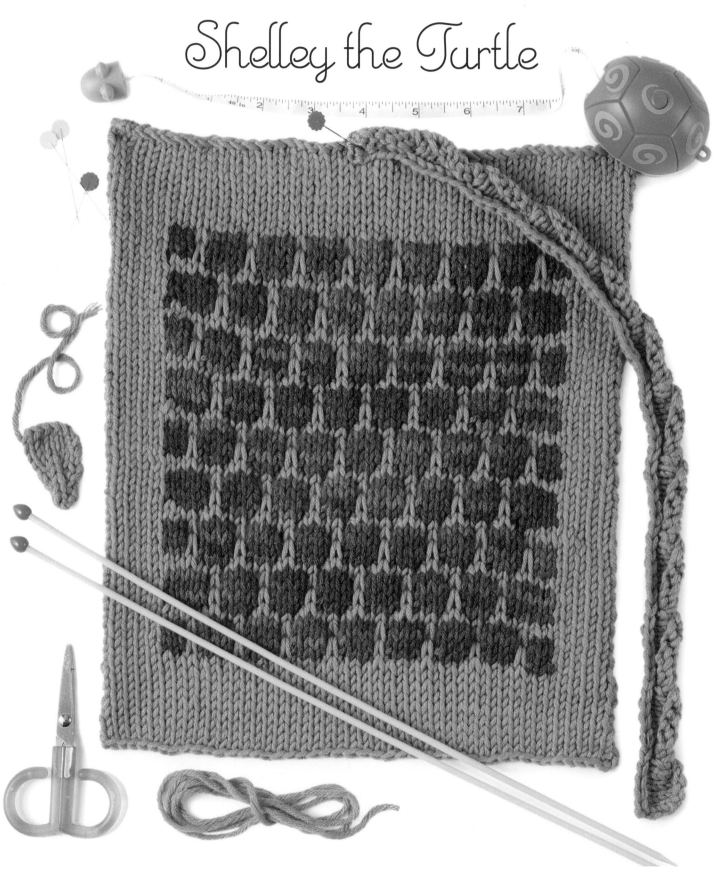

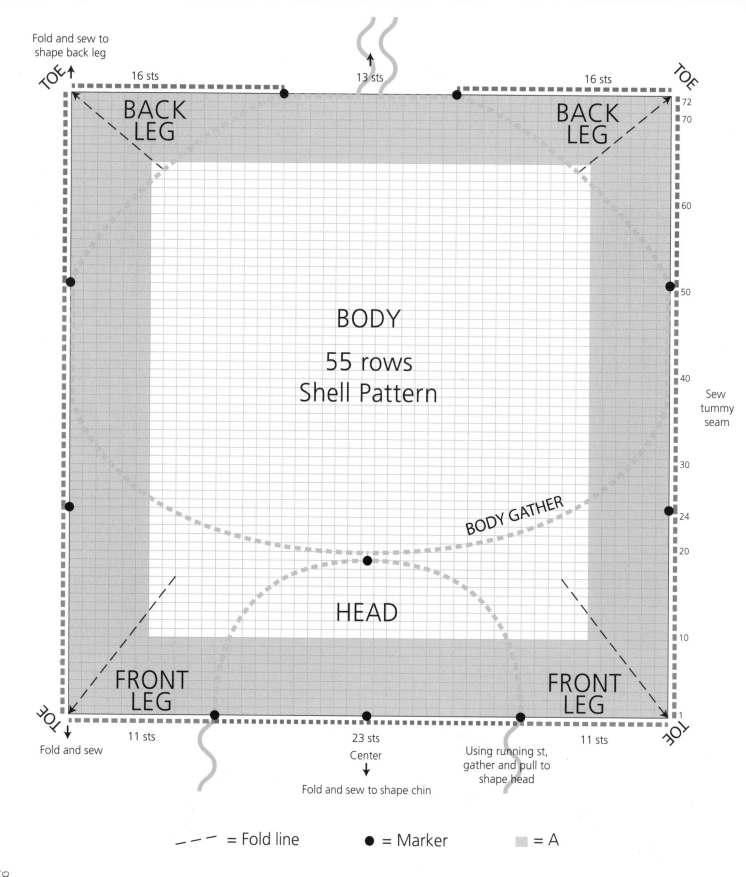

Fold and sew to shape back leg

TOE ↑

16 sts

13 sts ↑

16 sts

TOE

BACK LEG

BACK LEG

72
70

60

50

BODY

55 rows
Shell Pattern

40

Sew tummy seam

30

BODY GATHER

24

20

HEAD

10

FRONT LEG

FRONT LEG

TOE ↓

11 sts

23 sts
Center
↓

11 sts

TOE

1

Fold and sew

Fold and sew to shape chin

Using running st, gather and pull to shape head

– – – = Fold line   ● = Marker   ▨ = A

Shelley can be knitted at any speed you wish. Just remember: Slow and steady wins the race!

Materials

- 1 3½oz/100g balls (each approx 210yd/193m) of Berroco Comfort (nylon/acrylic) each in #9740 Seedling (A) and #9839 Maine Woods (B) (4)
- One pair size 8 (5mm) needles, OR SIZE TO OBTAIN GAUGE
- Small amount of pink yarn for mouth
- Stitch markers and tapestry needle
- Small length of pink ribbon
- Polyester stuffing

Gauge

18 sts and 26 rows to 4"/10cm over St st using size 8 (5mm) needles.
TAKE TIME TO CHECK GAUGE.

Note

When working chart, use separate lengths (butterflies) of yarn for each block of color and when changing colors, twist yarns on WS to prevent holes in work.

Shell Pattern

(over a multiple of 4 sts plus 1)
Preparation row (RS) With A, knit.
Row 1 WS With A, purl.
Rows 2 and 4 With B, knit.
Rows 3 and 5 With B, purl.
Row 6 With A, k2, *drop next st off needle and unravel 4 rows down, picking up the color A st from Row 1 below, insert needle into this st and under the 4 loose strands of color B, and knit, catching the 4 loose strands behind st, k3; rep from *, end last rep k2.
Row 7 With A, purl.
Rows 8 and 10 With B, knit.
Rows 9 and 11 With B, purl.
Row 12 With A, k4, *drop next st, unravel and knit color A st from 5th row below as in row 6, k3; rep from *, end k1.

Square

(approx 10"/25.5cm square)

With A, cast on 45 sts. Beg with a k row, work in St st (k on RS, p on WS) for 9 rows.
Beg shell pat
Row 1 (WS) With A, knit (row 1 of shell pat).
Row 2 (RS) With A, p6, join B and p33 (row 2 of shell pat), join 2nd ball of A and k6. Cont in patterns as established, keeping first st and last 6 sts in St st and center 33 sts in shell pat, until 12 rows of pat have been worked 4 times, then work rows 1–7 once more. Break B and cont in St st over all sts with A only for 8 rows. Bind off.

Shell Strip

Note If using a different weight yarn, you may need to adjust the number of cast on sts so that the strip fits around the body.
With A, cast on 70 sts. Work St st for 4 rows.
Next row (RS) *K5, rotate left-hand needle counter clockwise 360 degrees; rep from * to end. Bind off.

Tail

Cast on 5 sts, work in St st for 8 rows.
Row 9 (RS) K1, sl 1, k2tog, psso (SK2P), k1.
Row 10 P3. **Row 11** SK2P. Secure last st.

- -

Assembly

Lay square on a flat surface.
Mark center 23 sts along cast-on edge. Mark center st, measure up 18 rows from center st and place another marker. Cut a piece of color A approx 25"/63.5cm long and sew running sts to outline the head, foll the diagram for placement and leaving a long length at both ends. Mark the center 13 sts along bound-off edge. Cut a piece of color A approx 50"/127cm long and sew running sts along these sts, leaving a long length at both ends. Place markers along each side edge at 24 rows from cast-on to mark each front leg, 22 rows from bound-off edges to mark each back leg.

Head

Pull both ends of the running-st yarn that marked the head, gathering the fabric until the outer edges meet at the center, then tie the ends in a double knot tightly. Stuff the head firmly. Fold head in half and sew cast-on sts tog for chin seam.

Front Legs

Fold one front leg so that side edges meet (blue dotted lines) and form a point at the outer edge (toe), easing the longer edge into the shorter edge and pin the edges together. Sew the side edges together.
Fold and sew the other front leg in same way. Stuff the legs firmly.

Back Legs

Fold one back leg so that side edges meet (green dotted lines) and form a point at the outer edge and pin the edges together. Sew the side edges together. Fold and sew the other back leg in same way. Stuff the legs firmly.

Body

Stuff and shape the shell. Pull both ends of the running-st yarn that marked the body, gathering the fabric slightly, then tie the ends in a double knot tightly.

Tummy

Pin the remaining two sides together and with A, sew the tummy seam from tail to neck, gathering slightly. Pin shell strip around body and sew. Sew tail to bottom.

Finishing Details

With B, embroider French knots for eyes. With pink yarn, embroider mouth, with B, embroider another line below the pink line. Tie ribbon in a bow around the neck. ❦

1 Sew running stitches with tapestry needle following the outlines on the diagram. A contrast color is used here for clarity only.

2 Be sure to leave long lengths of yarn at either end of the running stitches to use for pulling and gathering the fabric.

3 To shape the head, pull on both ends of the yarn and gather the fabric until the outer edges meet.

4 Tie the ends very tightly into a double knot. Do not cut the ends, as they can be used later for seaming.

5 Stuff the head firmly, but not so much that the sts pull apart and show the stuffing.

6 Fold and pin the cast-on edges of the underside (or chin) together, then sew the chin seam.

7

Fold the sides of the legs together, stitches to rows, easing the longer side into the shorter side if necessary.

8

Pin the edges in place, then sew the leg seams.

9

Shown here is the finished head and the sewn front legs before stuffing.

10

Stuff the front legs firmly. Use a blunt tapestry needle to push up the stuffing into the point of the leg to form the toe.

11

Sew the back legs in the same manner as the front legs, pinning in place before seaming.

12

Once the two back legs are pinned in place, sew the back leg seams, easing the edges together if necessary.

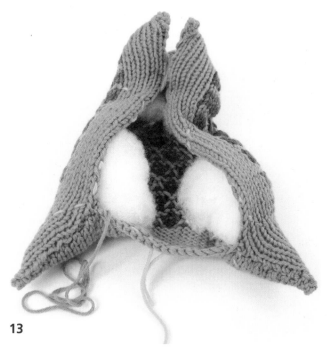

13

Stuff the back legs firmly. The more stuffing, the firmer the animal.

14

Stuff the remaining body, shaping to create a smooth shell. Then pull the two yarn ends from the running sts and gather the fabric slightly.

15

Pin the remaining two sides together and sew the tummy seam from tail to neck, gathering slightly as you sew.

16

Pin the shell piece around the body as shown, and sew the bound-off edge to the shell.

Callie the Cat

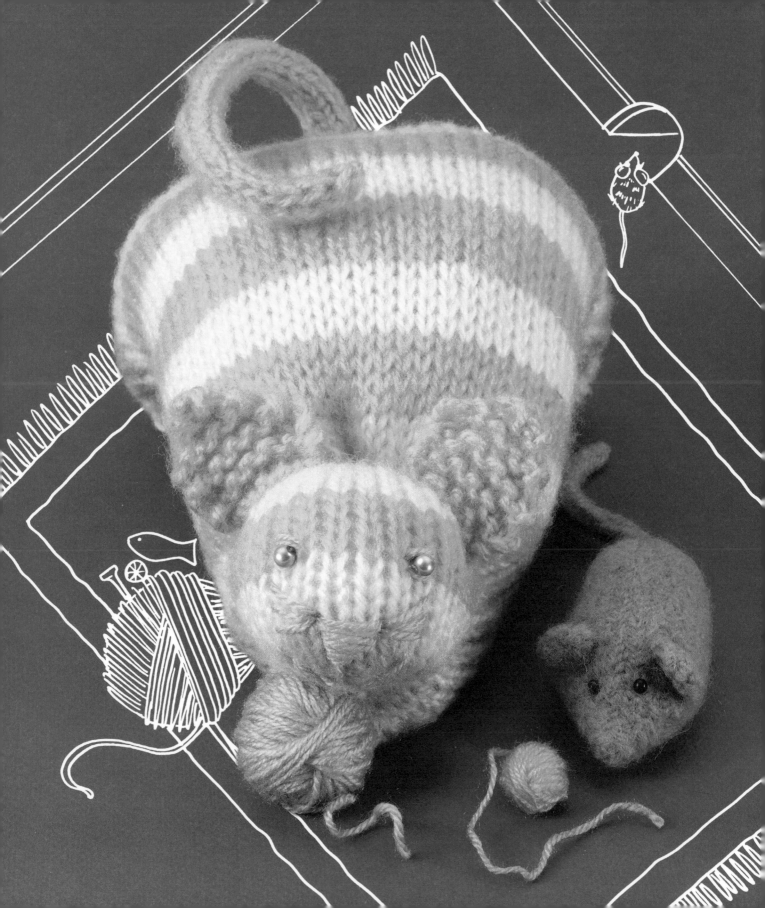

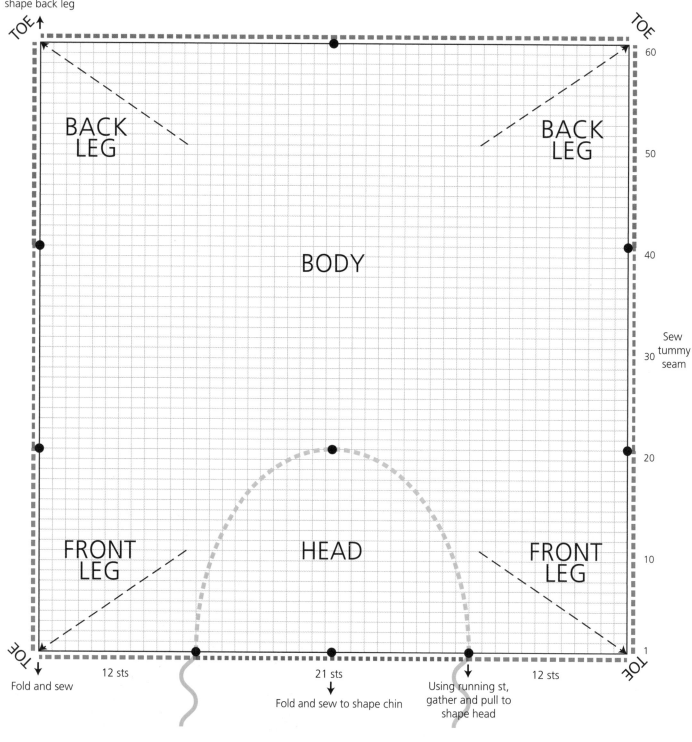

Fold and sew to
shape back leg

TOE

BACK LEG

BACK LEG

TOE

60

50

BODY

40

Sew
tummy
seam

30

20

FRONT LEG

HEAD

FRONT LEG

10

TOE

1

TOE

12 sts

21 sts

12 sts

Fold and sew

Fold and sew to shape chin

Using running st,
gather and pull to
shape head

─ ─ ─ = Fold line   ● = Marker

Callie the Cat

Callie and her kitty friends love yarn, and they'll help you purr-fect a few knitting techniques.

Materials
- **1 3oz/85g skein (each approx 185yd/170m) of Lion Brand Yarn Vanna's Complement (acrylic) each in #98 Fisherman (A) and #158 Mustard (B)** (4)
- **One pair size 9 (5.5mm) needles, OR SIZE TO OBTAIN GAUGE**
- **Two size 8 (5mm) double-pointed needles (dpn) for tail only**
- **Small amount of pink and green yarn for face embroidery**
- **2 beads for eyes**
- **Stitch markers**
- **Polyester stuffing**
- **Tapestry needle**

Gauge
16 sts and 22 rows to 4"/10cm over St st using size 9 (5.5mm) needles.
TAKE TIME TO CHECK GAUGE.

Stripe Pattern
*4 rows A, 4 rows B; rep from * (8 rows) for stripe pat.

Square
(approx 11"/28cm square)
With A, cast on 45 sts.
Work in St st (k on RS, p on WS) and stripe pat for 60 rows, ending with 4 rows A. Bind off with A.

Ears (make 2)
With B, cast on 7 sts.
Rows 1–4 Knit.
Row 5 Ssk, k to last 2 sts, k2tog—5 sts.
Row 6 Knit.
Row 7 Rep row 5—3 sts.
Row 8 SK2P.
Secure last st, leaving an end for attaching.

Tail
With dpn and B, cast on 4 sts.
*Row 1 (RS) Knit. Do *not* turn work.
Slide the sts back to the opposite end of needle to work next row from RS.
Pull yarn tightly from the end of the row.
Rep from * for approx. 6½"/16.5cm.
Bind off, leaving an end for attaching.

Assembly
Lay square on a flat surface. Mark the center 21 sts along cast-on edge. Mark center st, measure up 20 rows from center st and place another marker. Cut a piece of yarn approx 25"/63.5cm long and sew running sts to outline the head, following the diagram for placement and leaving a long length at both ends.
Place markers along each side edge at 20 rows from cast-on and bound-off edges to mark one half of each leg. Mark the center st along bound-off edge to mark other half of each back leg.

Head
Pull both ends of the running-st yarn that marked the head, gathering the fabric until the outer edges meet at the center, then tie the ends in a double knot tightly. Stuff the head firmly. Fold head in half and sew cast-on sts tog for chin seam.

Front Legs
Fold one front leg so that side edges (blue dotted lines) meet and form a point at the outer edge (toe), easing the longer side into the shorter side, and pin the edges together. Sew the side edges together. Fold and sew the other front leg in same way. Stuff the legs firmly.

Back Legs
Fold one back leg so that side edges (green dotted lines) meet at the center marked st and form a point at the outer edge (toe) easing the longer side into the shorter side, and pin the edges together. Sew the side edges together. Fold and sew the other back leg in same way. Stuff the legs firmly.

Tummy
Stuff the remainder of the body firmly. Pin the remaining two sides together and sew the tummy seam.

Finishing Details
Sew ears to head, leaving approx 1½"/4cm between the ears (use photo as a guide). Sew tail to top of butt.
Sew on beads for eyes. With green yarn, embroider straight sts around the eyes. With pink yarn, embroider nose with satin st in center of face, then embroider mouth with straight sts. With green yarn, embroider whiskers with straight sts on either side of the nose. ❀

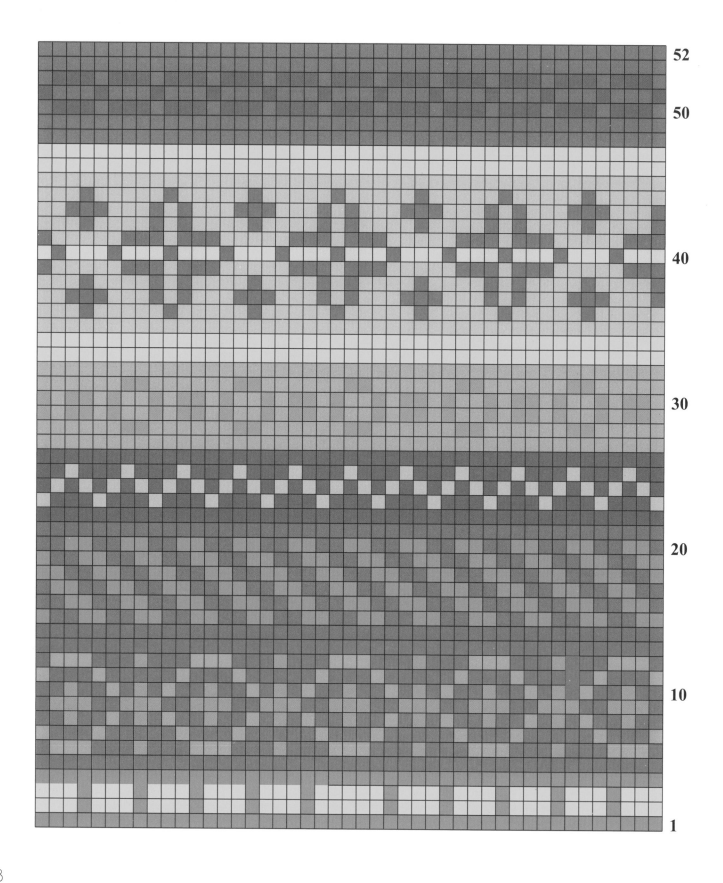

The Fair Isle Cat

Materials
- 1 package of 8 .35oz/10g skeins (each approx 28yd/20m) of Lion Brand Yarn Bonbons (acrylic) in #610 Brights: Orange-Red (A), Yellow (B), Turquoise (C), Lime (D), Magenta (E), Purple (F), Pink (G) and Orange (H) (2)
- One pair size 6 (4mm) needles, OR SIZE TO OBTAIN GAUGE
- Two size 5 (3.75mm) double-pointed needles (dpn) for tail only
- 2 beads for eyes
- Stitch markers
- Polyester stuffing
- Tapestry needle

Gauge
23 sts and 26 rows to 4"/10cm over St st and chart pat using size 6 (4mm) needles. TAKE TIME TO CHECK GAUGE.

Square
(approx 8"/20.5cm square)
With A, cast on 45 sts.
Work in St st (k on RS, p on WS) and chart pat for 52 rows. Bind off with E.

Ears (make 2)
With D, cast on 7 sts. Work same as Callie the Cat.

COLOR KEY
- Orange-Red (A)
- Yellow (B)
- Turquoise (C)
- Lime (D)
- Magenta (E)
- Purple (F)
- Pink (G)
- Orange (H)

Tail
With dpn and F, cast on 4 sts. Work same as Callie the Cat.

Assembly
Lay square on a flat surface.
Mark the center 21 sts along cast-on edge. Measure up 17 rows from center st on cast-on edge and place another marker. Cut a piece of yarn approx 25"/63.5cm long and sew running sts to outline the head, referring to the diagram on page 26 for placement and leaving a long length at both ends.

Place markers along each side edge at 17 rows from cast-on and bound-off edges to mark one half of each leg. Mark the center st along bound-off edge to mark other half of each back leg.

Complete assembly same as Callie the Cat.

Finishing Details
Sew ears to head, leaving approx ¾"/2cm between the ears (use photo as a guide). Sew tail to top of butt.
Sew on beads for eyes.
With E, embroider nose with satin st in center of face, then embroider mouth with straight sts. With D, embroider whiskers with straight sts on either side of the nose. ✿

THE QUILTED
DAISY CAT

THE BEADED CAT

THE FAIR ISLE CAT

THE SEED STITCH CAT

The Quilted Daisy Stitch Cat

Materials
- 1 3½oz/100g skein (each approx 273yd/250m) of Premier Yarns Primo (acrylic) each in #0010 Turquoise ⓛ
- Small amounts of a variety of yarn colors of your choice for embroidery
- One pair size 7 (4.5mm) needles, OR SIZE TO OBTAIN GAUGE
- Two size 6 (4mm) double-pointed needles (dpn) for tail only
- 2 beads for eyes
- Stitch markers and tapestry needle
- Polyester stuffing

Gauge
20 sts and 24 rows to 4"/10cm over quilt st using size 7 (4.5mm) needles.
TAKE TIME TO CHECK GAUGE.

Quilt Stitch
(over a multiple of 14 sts)
Rows 1, 3 and 5 (WS) K3, *p8, k6; rep from *, end p8, k3.
Rows 2 and 4 Knit.
Row 6 K2, *p2, k6, p2, k4; rep from *, end last rep k2.
Row 7 P3, *k2, p4, k2, p6; rep from *, end last rep p3.
Row 8 K4, *p2, p2, k8; rep from *, end last rep k4.
Row 9 P5, *k4, p10; rep from *, end k4, p5.
Row 10 Rep row 8.
Row 11 Rep row 7.
Row 12 Rep row 6.
Rep rows 1–12 for quilt st.

Square
(approx 8"/20.5cm square)
Cast on 42 sts. Work in quilt st for 48 rows. Bind off.
With desired colors, work a 5-petal flower, using lazy daisy st in center of diamonds at top of head, along center of back and on each leg (see photo).

Ears and Tail
Work same as Callie the Cat.

. . . .

Assembly
Lay square on a flat surface.
Mark the center 20 sts along cast-on edge. Measure up 16 rows from center st on cast-on edge and place another marker. Cut a piece of yarn approx 25"/63.5cm long and sew running sts to outline the head, referring to the diagram on page 26 for placement and leaving a long length at both ends.
Place markers along each side edge at 16 rows from cast-on and bound-off edges to mark one half of each leg.
Mark the center st along bound-off edge to mark other half of each back leg.

Complete assembly same as Callie the Cat.

Finishing Details
Sew ears to head, leaving approx ½"/1.5cm between the ears (use photo as a guide).
Sew tail to top of butt.
Sew on beads for eyes.
With desired color, embroider nose with satin st in center of face, then embroider mouth with straight sts.
With desired color, embroider whiskers with straight sts on either side of the nose. ❀

. . . .

The Beaded Cat

Materials
- 1 3½oz/100g skein (each approx 220yd/200m) of Cascade Yarns 220 Superwash (superwash wool) in #851 Lime (A) ④
- 1 .88oz/25g ball (each approx 229yd/210m) of Rowan Kidsilk Haze (mohair/silk) in #642 Ghost (B) ②
- Small amount of pink yarn colors to embroider face
- One pair size 8 (5mm) needles, OR SIZE TO OBTAIN GAUGE
- Two size 7 (4.5mm) double-pointed needles (dpn) for tail only
- 1 mixed bag of plastic crystal beads (found in craft stores)
- 2 beads for eyes
- Stitch markers
- Polyester stuffing
- Tapestry needle

Gauge
18 sts and 22 rows to 4"/10cm over St st using size 8 (5mm) needles and 1 strand each of A and B held tog.
TAKE TIME TO CHECK GAUGE.

Note
Work with 1 strand each A and B held together throughout.

Square
(approx 8"/20.5cm square)
String beads onto B. **Note** Slide beads down onto yarn until needed.
With 1 strand each A and B held tog, cast on 35 sts.
Purl 1 row, knit 1 row.
Work in bead pat as foll:
Row 1 (WS) K2, *slip bead up to needle and k1 (push bead to back of work so that it will show on the RS of the piece), k1; rep from * to last 2 sts, k2.
Row 2 Purl.
Row 3 K3, *slip bead and k1 as before, k1; rep from * to last 3 sts, k3.
Row 4 Purl.
Rep last 4 rows ten times more.
Knit 1 row, purl 1 row. Bind off knitwise.

Ears
String 14 beads on B. Holding A and B tog, cast on 7 sts.
Row 1 (RS) Knit.
Row 2 K1, [slip bead and k1 (push bead to back), k1] 3 times.
Row 3 Knit.
Row 4 [Slip bead and k1 (push bead to back), k1] 3 times, sl bead and k1.
Row 5 Knit.
Row 6 Rep row 2.

THE CABLE CAT

THE DOMINO CAT

Row 7 Ssk, k3, k2tog—5 sts.
Row 8 [Slip bead and k1, k1] twice, slip bead and k1.
Row 9 Ssk, k1, k2tog—3 sts.
Row 10 K1, sl bead and k1, k1.
Row 11 Slip 1, k2tog, psso.

Tail
String 8 beads on B. Holding A and B tog, with dpn, cast on 5 sts. Work I-cord as foll:
*Row 1 (RS) K2, slip bead and k1, k2. Do *not* turn work. Slide the sts back to the opposite end of needle to work next row from RS.
Rows 2 and 3 (RS) K5. Do *not* turn work. Slide the sts back to the opposite end of needle to work next row from RS.

Rep from * (3 rows) for approx. 5"/12.5cm.
Next row (RS) K1, SK2P, k1—3 sts. Do *not* turn work. Slide the sts back to the opposite end of needle to work next row from RS.
Next row (RS) Sl 1, p2 tog, psso. Secure last st.

· ·

Assembly
Lay square on a flat surface. Mark the center 13 sts along cast-on edge. Measure up 14 rows from center st on cast-on edge and place another marker. Cut a piece of yarn approx 25"/63.5cm long and sew running sts to outline the head, referring to the diagram on page 26 for placement and

leaving a long length at both ends. Place markers along each side edge at 14 rows from cast-on and bound-off edges to mark one half of each leg. Mark the center st along bound-off edge to mark other half of each back leg.

Complete assembly same as Callie the Cat.

Finishing Details
Sew ears to head, leaving approx ½"/1.5cm between the ears (use photo as a guide). Sew tail to top of butt.
Sew on beads for eyes. With pink yarn, embroider nose with satin st in center of face, then embroider mouth with straight sts. ❀

· ·

The Seed Stitch Cat

Materials
• 1 3½oz/100g skein (each approx 220yd/200m) of Cascade Yarns 220 Superwash Effects (superwash wool) in #09 Autumn (4)
• Small amounts of brown and lime green yarn and beige embroidery floss for face embroidery
• One pair size 7 (4.5mm) needles, OR SIZE TO OBTAIN GAUGE
• Two size 6 (4mm) double-pointed needles (dpn) for tail only
• Stitch markers
• Polyester stuffing
• Tapestry needle

Gauge
20 sts and 32 rows to 4"/10cm over seed st using size 7 (4.5mm) needles.
TAKE TIME TO CHECK GAUGE.

Seed Stitch
(over an odd number of sts)
Row 1 (RS) K1, *p1, k1; rep from * to end.
Row 2 (WS) Rep row 1.
Rep rows 1 and 2 for seed st.

Square
(approx 9"/23cm square)
Cast on 45 sts. Work in seed st for 72 rows. Bind off.

Ears and Tail
Work same as Callie the Cat.

Assembly
Lay square on a flat surface. Mark the center 21 sts along cast-on edge. Measure up 24 rows from center st on cast-on edge and place another marker. Cut a piece of yarn approx 25"/63.5cm long and sew running sts to outline the head, referring to the diagram on page 26 for placement and leaving a long length at both ends.
Place markers along each side edge at 24 rows from cast-on and bound-off edges to mark one half of each leg
Mark the center st along bound-off edge to mark other half of each back leg.

Complete assembly same as Callie the Cat.

Finishing Details
Sew ears to head, leaving approx 1"/2.5cm between the ears (use photo as a guide). Sew tail to top of butt.
With green yarn, embroider French knots for eyes. With brown yarn, embroider nose with satin st in center of face, then embroider mouth with straight sts. With embroidery floss, embroider whiskers with straight sts on either side of the nose. ❀

The Cable Cat

Materials

- 1 3½oz/100g skein (each approx 205yd/189m) of Berroco Weekend (acrylic/cotton) in #5936 Violet (4)
- Small amounts of turquoise, lime green and pink yarn for face embroidery
- One pair size 7 (4.5mm) needles, OR SIZE TO OBTAIN GAUGE
- Two size 6 (4mm) double-pointed needles (dpn) for tail only
- Cable needle (cn)
- Stitch markers
- Polyester stuffing
- Tapestry needle

Gauge

20 sts and 32 rows to 4"/10cm over cable pat using size 7 (4.5mm) needles.
TAKE TIME TO CHECK GAUGE.

Cable Pattern

(over a multiple of 6 sts plus 2)

Row 1 (RS) P2, *k4, p2; rep from * to end.
Rows 2, 4, 6 and 8 (WS) K2, *p4, k2; rep from * to end.
Row 3 P2, *sl 2 sts to cn and hold to *front*, k2, k2 from cn, p2; rep from * to end.
Rows 5 and 7 Rep row 1.
Rep rows 1–8 for cable pat.

Square

(approx 9"/23cm square)
Cast on 62 sts. Work in cable pat for 72 rows. Bind off.

Ears and Tail

Work same as Callie the Cat.

. . . .

Assembly

Lay square on a flat surface. Mark the center 21 sts along cast-on edge. Measure up 24 rows from center st on cast-on edge and place another marker. Cut a piece of yarn approx 25"/63.5cm long and sew running sts to outline the head, referring to the diagram on page 26 for placement and leaving a long length at both ends. Place markers along each side edge at 24 rows from cast-on and bound-off edges to mark one half of each leg. Mark the center st along bound-off edge to mark other half of each back leg.

Complete assembly same as Callie the Cat.

Finishing Details

Sew ears to head, leaving approx 1"/2.5cm between the ears (use photo as a guide). Sew tail to top of butt.
With turquoise yarn, embroider French knots for eyes. With lime green yarn, embroider straight sts around eyes. With pink yarn, embroider nose with satin st in center of face, then embroider mouth with straight stitches. With turquoise yarn, embroider whiskers with straight sts on either side of the nose. ✿

. . . .

The Domino Cat

Materials

- 1 1¾oz/50g hank (each approx 175yd/158m) of Koigu Wool Designs KPM (merino wool) in #1003 Solid Blue (MC) (2)
- 1 1¾oz/50g hank (each approx 175yd/158m) of Koigu Wool Designs KPPPM (merino wool) in #P518 Blue Multi (CC) (2)
- Small amount of pink for face embroidery
- One pair size 6 (4mm) needles, OR SIZE TO OBTAIN GAUGE
- Two size 5 (3.75mm) double-pointed needles (dpn) for tail only
- 2 beads for eyes
- Stitch markers
- Polyester stuffing
- Tapestry needle

Gauge

One mitered square to 1¾"/4.5cm using size 6 (4mm) needles.
TAKE TIME TO CHECK GAUGE.

Note

Larger size needles and looser gauge than recommended for this yarn was used.

Stitch Glossary

S2KP Slip 2 sts as if to k2tog, k1, pass the 2 slipped sts over the k1.
S2PP Slip 2 sts as if to p2tog tbl, p1, pass the 2 slipped sts over the p1.

Mitered Square

(over 19 sts)
Note Carry color not in use along edge of work to avoid cutting and weaving in ends later.
Row 1 (WS) With MC, knit.
Row 2 With CC, k8, S2KP, k8—17 sts.
Row 3 With CC, k8, p1, k8.
Row 4 With MC, k7, S2KP, k7—15 sts.
Row 5 With MC, k7, p1, k7.
Row 6 With CC, k6, S2KP, k6—13 sts.
Row 7 With CC, k6, p1, k6.
Row 8 With MC, k5, S2KP, k5—11 sts.
Row 9 With MC, k5, p1, k5.
Row 10 With CC, k4, S2KP, k4—9 sts.
Row 11 With CC, k4, p1, k4.
Row 12 With MC, k3, S2KP, k3—7 sts.
Row 13 With MC, k3, p1, k3.
Row 14 With CC, k2, S2KP, k2—5 sts.
Row 15 With CC, k2, p1, k2.
Row 16 With MC, k1, S2KP, k1—3 sts.
Row 17 With MC, S2PP—1 st.
Do *not* fasten off unless otherwise indicated.

First Row of Squares

Square 1
With MC, cast on 19 sts using knitted cast-on. Work rows 1–17 of mitered square. The last st on needle counts as the first st for the next square.

Square 2
With the right side facing and MC, place the rem st from the previous square on RH needle, pick up and k 8 sts along the left side of square 1, pick up and k 1 st in the corner, cast on 9 sts—19 sts. Work rows 1–17 of mitered square.

Squares 3–6
Work same as square 2, picking up sts along adjoining squares (see diagram below).

Second Row of Squares

Square 7
With MC, cast on 9 sts, then with the right side facing pick up and k 10 sts along top edge of square 1—19 sts. Work rows 1–17 of mitered square.

Square 8
With the right side facing and MC, place the rem st from the previous square on RH needle, pick up and k 8 sts along left side of square 7, pick up and k 10 sts along top of square 2—19 sts. Work rows 1–17 of mitered square.

Squares 9–12
Work same as square 8, picking up sts along adjoining squares (see diagram).

Third–Sixth Row of Squares

Work same as second row of squares, picking up sts along adjoining squares.
The final square is 6 squares wide by 6 squares tall and measures approx 10½"/26.5cm.

Ears (make 2)

With MC, cast on 19 sts and work rows 1–17 of mitered square. Secure last st.

Tail

With dpn and MC, cast on 4 sts and work same as Callie the Cat, alternating 2 rows of MC and 2 rows of CC.

. . . .

Assembly

Lay square on a flat surface. Mark the center 2 squares (squares 3 and 4 on diagram). Measure up 2 squares from the center of the lower edge and place another marker. Cut a piece of yarn approx 25"/63.5cm long and sew running sts to outline the head, referring to the diagram on page 26 for placement and leaving a long length at both ends.
Place markers along each side edge at 2 squares up from the lower edge and 2 squares down from the top edge to mark one half of each leg. Mark the center along top edge to mark other half of each back leg.

Complete assembly same as Callie the Cat.

Finishing Details

Place markers for two ears near the top of the head, leaving approx 2"/5cm between the markers. To form the ears, fold one square in half so that the top and bottom points meet and the right side of the fabric is facing out. Sew side edges together to create a triangle. Center the folded edge at the marker and curve the outer ends inward to form a small arc.
Sew the ears in place (see photo as a guide). Sew tail to top of butt.
Sew on beads for eyes.
With pink yarn, embroider nose with satin st in center of face, then embroider mouth with straight sts.
With CC, embroider whiskers with straight sts on either side of the nose. ✽

Domino Cat Diagram

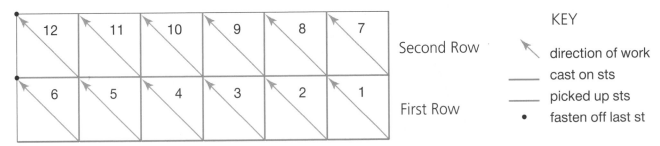

| 12 | 11 | 10 | 9 | 8 | 7 | Second Row |
| 6 | 5 | 4 | 3 | 2 | 1 | First Row |

KEY
↖ direction of work
— cast on sts
— picked up sts
• fasten off last st

Hugo the Hedgehog

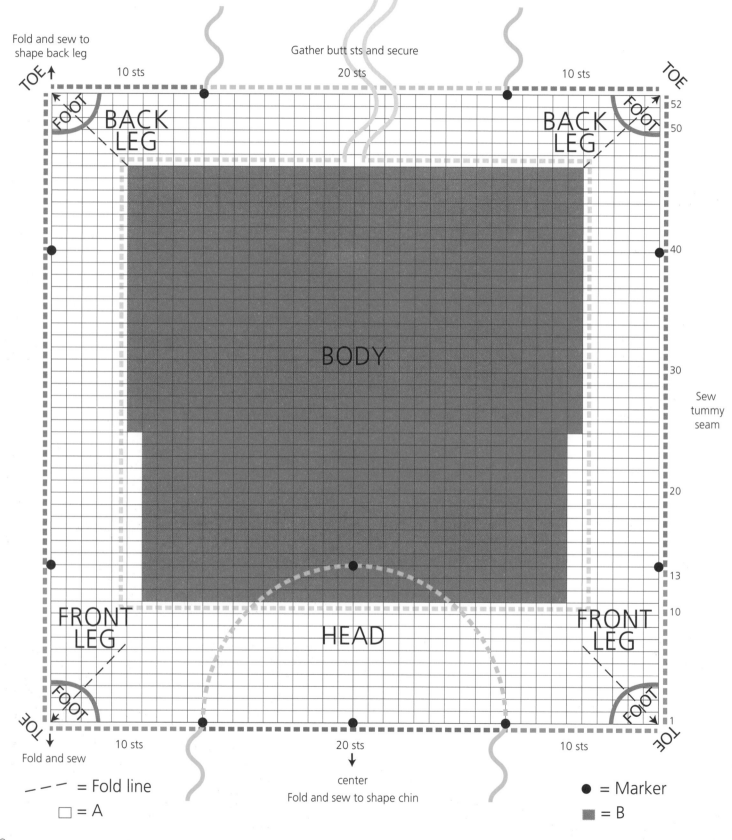

Fold and sew to shape back leg

Gather butt sts and secure

TOE↑

10 sts   20 sts   10 sts

TOE

FOOT

BACK LEG

BACK LEG

FOOT

52

50

40

BODY

Sew tummy seam

30

20

13

FRONT LEG

HEAD

FRONT LEG

FOOT

FOOT

10

TOE

TOE

10 sts   20 sts   10 sts

↓
Fold and sew

↓
center
Fold and sew to shape chin

– – – = Fold line

☐ = A

● = Marker

▨ = B

38

When asked a question, hedgehogs usually hedge the answer. Even so, these fellows are cute, they'll charm you.

Materials
- 1 3½oz/100g skein (each approx 170yd/156m) of Lion Brand Yarn Vanna's Choice (acrylic) in #101 Ecru (A) (4)
- 1 1¾oz/50g skein (each approx 47yd/43m) of Lion Brand Yarn Pelt (nylon/polyester) in #203 Fisher (B) (5)
- One pair size 9 (5.5mm) needles, OR SIZE TO OBTAIN GAUGE
- Small amount of black and pink yarn for face embroidery, small amount of light brown yarn for feet
- Stitch markers
- Polyester stuffing
- Tapestry needle

Gauge
16 sts and 20 rows to 4"/10cm over St st using 2 strands of Vanna's Choice held tog and size 9 (4.5mm) needles.
TAKE TIME TO CHECK GAUGE.

Note
When working chart, use separate lengths (butterflies) of yarn for each block of color and when changing colors, twist yarns on WS to prevent holes in work.

Square
(approx 10"/25.5cm square)
With 2 strands of A held tog, cast on 40 sts. Beg with a knit row, work in St st (k on RS, p on WS) for 10 rows.
Row 11 (RS) With A, k6; with B, k28; with another length (or butterfly) of A, k6.
Row 12 (WS) With A, p6; with B, p28; with another length (or butterfly) of A, p6.
Rows 13–24 Rep rows 11 and 12 six times.
Row 25 With A, k5; with B, k30; with another length (or butterfly) of A, k5.
Row 26 With A, p5; with B, p30; with

another length (or butterfly) of A, p5.
Rows 27–46 Rep rows 25 and 26 eleven times. Cut B and 2nd length of A.
Rows 47–52 With A only, work in St st. Bind off.

Ears (make 2)
With 2 strands of A held tog, cast on 6 sts. Knit 1 row.
Pass all sts over 1st st and off the needle one at a time.

- -

Assembly
Lay square on a flat surface.
Mark the center 20 sts along cast-on edge. Mark center st, measure up 13 rows from center st and place another marker. Cut a piece of color A approx 25"/63.5cm long and sew running sts to outline the head, following the diagram for placement and leaving a long length at both ends.
Mark the center 20 sts along bound-off edge. Cut a piece of color A and sew running sts along these sts for butt, leaving a long length at both ends (yellow dotted line).
Cut a piece of color A approx 50"/127cm long and sew running sts to outline the body (pink dotted line).
Place markers along each side edge at 13 rows from cast-on and bound-off edges to mark each leg.

Head
Pull both ends of the running-st yarn that marked the head, gathering the fabric until the outer edges meet at the center, then tie the ends in a double knot tightly. Stuff the head firmly.
Fold head in half, pin and sew cast-on sts tog for chin seam.

Body and Butt
Pull both ends of the running-st yarn that marked the body, gathering the fabric until the outer edges shape the back hump, then tie the ends in a double knot.
Pull tightly and secure end.
Work in same way for the butt.

Front Legs
Fold one front leg so that side edges meet (blue dotted lines) and form a point at the outer edge (toe), easing the longer edge into the shorter edge and pin the edges together. Sew the side edges together. Fold and sew the other front leg in same way. Stuff the legs tightly.

Back Legs
Fold one back leg so that side edges meet (green dotted lines) and form a point at the outer edge and pin the edges together Sew the side edges together.
Fold and sew the other back leg in same way. Stuff the legs tightly.

Tummy
Stuff the remainder of the body tightly. Pin the remaining two sides together and with A, sew the tummy seam from tail to neck gathering slightly.

Finishing Details
Sew ears to head, approx 1"/2.5cm apart. With black yarn, embroider French knots for eyes and satin st for nose and pull to shape a point.
With pink yarn, embroider mouth.
Wrap and tie light brown yarn around top of each leg to shape a foot. ❁

Amanda the Panda

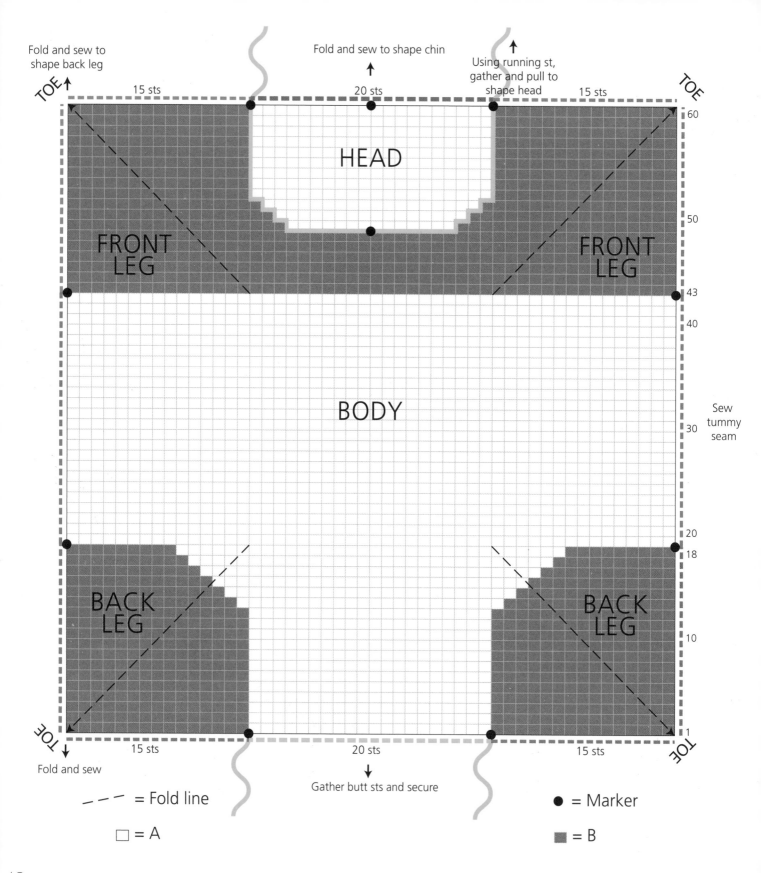

Fold and sew to shape back leg

Fold and sew to shape chin

Using running st, gather and pull to shape head

TOE

15 sts

20 sts

15 sts

TOE

60

HEAD

FRONT LEG

FRONT LEG

50

43

40

BODY

Sew tummy seam

30

20

18

BACK LEG

BACK LEG

10

1

TOE

TOE

15 sts

20 sts

15 sts

Fold and sew

Gather butt sts and secure

– – – = Fold line

● = Marker

□ = A

■ = B

Take a gander at Amanda, munching bamboo on her veranda. She just might be the happiest panda.

Materials
- 1 1¾oz/50g ball (each approx 104yd/95m) of Sirdar Ophelia (acrylic/nylon /polyester) each in #107 Bunny (A) and #100 Black (B) **(4)**
- One pair size 9 (5.5mm) needles, **OR SIZE TO OBTAIN GAUGE**
- 2 small black beads for eyes
- Stitch markers
- Polyester stuffing
- Tapestry needle

Gauge
20 sts and 24 rows to 4"/10cm over St st using size 9 (5.5mm) needles.
TAKE TIME TO CHECK GAUGE

Note
When working chart, use separate lengths (butterflies) of yarn for each block of color and when changing colors, twist yarns on WS to prevent holes in work.

Square
(approx 10"/25.5cm square)
With B, cast on 15 sts, with A cast on 20 sts, with B cast on 15 sts—50 sts in total.
Work in St st working colors as foll:
Rows 1–12 Cont in established colors from cast-on row.
Row 13 (RS) K14 B, k22 A, k14 B.
Cont to work colors are shown on diagram, through row 60.
Bind off, matching colors.

Ears
With B, cast on 18 sts.
Knit 3 rows.
Join A and knit 1 row.
*Pass 2nd st over first st and off the needle; rep from * until 1 st remains.
Secure last st.

Tail
With A, cast on 5 sts. Work St st for 1"/2.5cm.
Next row (RS) Ssk, k1, k2tog—3 sts.
Next row (WS) Slip 1, p2tog, psso.
Secure last st.
Sew tail seam.

. . . .

Assembly
Lay square on a flat surface.
Mark center 20 sts along cast-on edge. Cut a piece of color A approx 15"/38cm long and sew running sts along these sts for the butt, leaving a long length at both ends.
Mark the center 20 sts along bound-off edge.
Mark center st, measure down 18 rows from center st and place another marker.
Cut a piece of color A approx 25"/63.5cm long and sew running sts to outline the head, following the diagram for placement and leaving a long length at both ends.
Place markers along each side edge at 18 rows from cast-on and bound-off edges to mark half of each leg.

Head
Pull both ends of the running-st yarn that marked the head, gathering the fabric until the outer edges meet at the center, then tie the ends in a double knot tightly. Stuff the head firmly. Fold head in half, pin and sew cast-on sts tog for chin seam.

Front Legs
Fold one front leg so that side edges meet (blue dotted lines) and form a point at the outer edge (toe), easing the longer edge into the shorter edge and pin the edges together. Sew the side edges together. Fold and sew the other front leg in same way. Stuff the legs firmly.

Butt
Pull both ends of the yarn that marked the butt, gathering the fabric, then tie the ends in a double knot.
Be sure that the yarn is pulled tightly.

Back Legs
Fold one back leg so that side edges meet (green dotted lines) and form a point at the outer edge and pin the edges together. Sew the side edges together. Fold and sew the other back leg in same way. Stuff the legs firmly.

Tummy
Stuff the remainder of the body firmly. Pin the remaining two sides together and with A, sew the tummy seam.

Finishing Details
Sew ears to head, leaving approx 1½"/4cm between the ears (use photo as a guide). With B, embroider straight sts to shape the eyes. Sew bead in center of straight sts. With B, embroider nose with satin st in center of face, then embroider mouth with straight sts. ❀

Sheldon the Shark

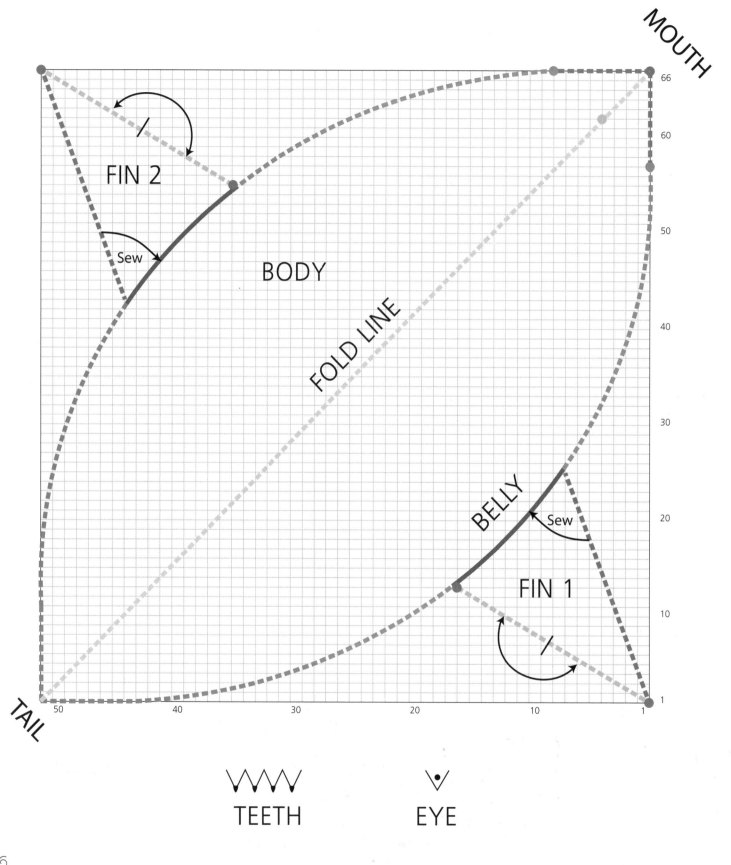

MOUTH

FIN 2

Sew

BODY

FOLD LINE

BELLY

Sew

FIN 1

TAIL

50 40 30 20 10 1

66
60
50
40
30
20
10
1

VVVV
TEETH

EYE

46

Sheldon's so lifelike you'll want to take your time as you knit so you don't get bit.

Materials
- 1 3½oz/100g balls (each approx 210yd/193m) of Berroco Comfort (nylon/acrylic) in #9774 Cobalt (4)
- One pair each sizes 5 and 8 (3.75 and 5mm) needles,
OR SIZE TO OBTAIN GAUGE
- Small amount of white yarn for face embroidery
- 2 small black beads for eyes
- Stitch markers
- Polyester stuffing
- Tapestry needle

Gauge
20 sts and 26 rows to 4"/10cm over woven st using size 8 (5mm) needles.
TAKE TIME TO CHECK GAUGE.

Woven Stitch
Row 1 (RS) K1, *sl 1 wyif, bring yarn to back and k1; rep from * to end.
Row 2 Purl.
Row 3 K2, *sl 1 wyif, bring yarn to back and k1; rep from * to last st, k1.
Row 4 Purl.
Rep rows 1–4 for woven st.

Square
(approx 10"/25.5cm square)
With larger needles, cast on 51 sts.
Work in woven st for 66 rows or until piece measures 10"/25.5cm from beg. Bind off.

Top Fin (make 2)
With smaller needles, cast on 1 st.
Row 1 (RS) Kfb—2 sts.
Row 2 and all WS rows Purl.
Row 3 Kfb, k1—3 sts.
Row 5 Kfb, k1, kfb—5 sts.
Row 7 Kfb, k3, kfb—7 sts.
Row 9 Kfb, k5, kfb—9 sts.

Row 11 Kfb, k7, kfb—11 sts.
Row 13 Kfb, k9, kfb—13 sts.
Row 15 Kfb, k11, kfb—15 sts.
Row 17 K15.
Bind off. Sew 2 fins tog, stuff lightly.

Top Tail Fin (make 2)
With smaller needles, cast on 1 st.
Row 1 (WS) Purl.
Row 2 Knit.
Row 3 Purl.
Work rows 1–9 as for Top Fin—9 sts.
Work even in St st (k on RS, p on WS) until fin measures 4"/10cm from beg. Bind off.
Sew 2 fins tog and stuff lightly.

Bottom Tail Fin (make 2)
With smaller needles, cast on 1 st.
Work rows 1–3 as for Top Fin—3 sts.
Row 4 Purl.
Row 5 Knit.
Row 6 Purl.
Work rows 5–11 as for Top Fin—11 sts.

Cont in St st until fin measures 2½"/6.5cm from beg. Bind off.
Sew 2 fins tog and stuff lightly.

....

Assembly
With RS together, fold square in half (pink line on diagram) to make a triangle.
Sew blue lines on diagram leaving purple line open. Turn to RS. Pull fins through purple section opening. Stuff body.
Sew mouth closed by sewing from blue dot to blue dot on diagram, fold point inside from green dot to orange dot.
Fold 2 side blue dots together and tack together to shape mouth.
Lay fins apart. Sew purple line for belly closed. Fold red dot of fin 1 tip to red dot on belly, sew underside of fin to purple line. Sew bound-off edges and repeat for fin 2, sewing in opposite direction.
Sew remaining fins to shark following photo.
With white yarn, embroider teeth following diagram.
Make 2 V's for eyes, sew bead to each eye. ✿

Caleb the Bullfrog

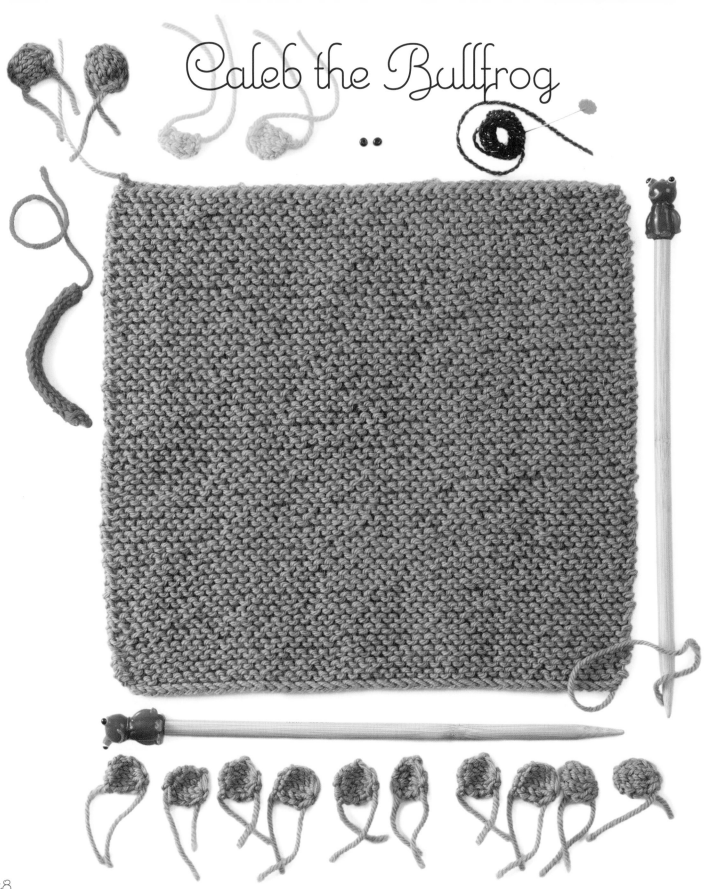

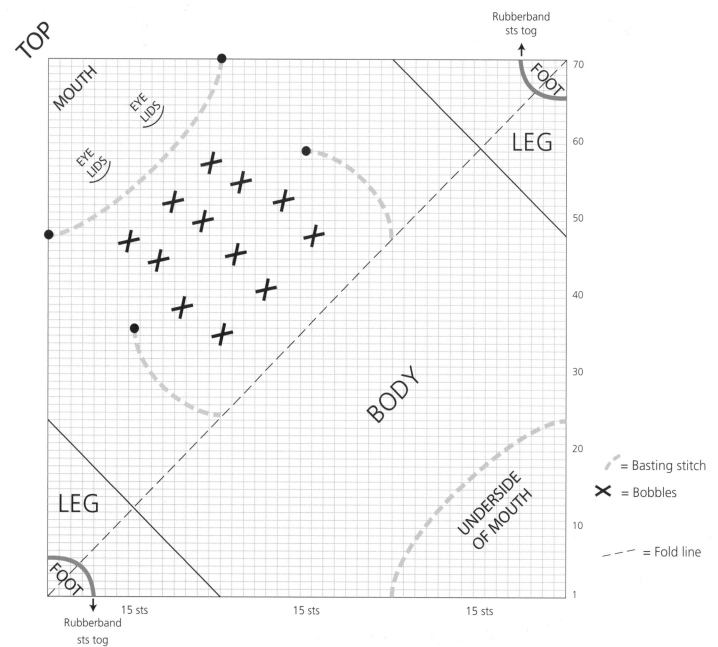

= Basting stitch

✗ = Bobbles

‑ ‑ ‑ = Fold line

Caleb may look shy, but he's the ultimate flycatcher with the quickest tongue around.

Materials
- 1 3½oz/100g ball (each approx 220yd/200m) of Cascade 220 Superwash (superwash wool) in #841 Moss (4)
- One pair size 8 (5mm) needles, OR SIZE TO OBTAIN GAUGE
- Two size 5 (3.75mm) double-pointed needles (dpn) for tongue and bobbles
- Small amount of red, yellow and black yarn for face, tongue and eyes
- 2 small black beads for eyes
- 2 small rubber bands
- Stitch markers
- Polyester stuffing
- Tapestry needle

Gauge
18 sts and 28 rows to 4"/10cm over garter st using size 8 (5mm) needles.
TAKE TIME TO CHECK GAUGE

Square
(approx 10"/25.5cm square)
With size 8 (5mm) needles, cast on 45 sts.
Work in garter st (k every row) for 70 rows.
Piece should measures 10"/25.5cm from beg.
Bind off.

Bobbles
(Make 14: 12 in Moss for body, 2 in yellow for eyes)
Make a slipknot onto one dpn.
Row 1 (RS) Knit into front, back, front, back and front of st—5 sts.
Row 2 Purl.
Row 3 Knit.
Row 4 Purl.
Row 5 Ssk, k1, k2tog—3 sts.
Row 6 P3tog. Secure last st.
Leave a tail for attaching.

Tongue
With dpn and red yarn cast on 4 sts.
***Row 1 (RS)** Knit. Do *not* turn work.
Slide the sts back to the opposite end of needle to work next row from RS.
Pull yarn tightly from the end of the row.
Rep from * for 2½"/6.5cm. [K2tog] twice, p2tog. Secure last st.

Eyelids (make 2)
Make a slipknot onto one dpn.
Row 1 (RS) Knit into front, back and front of st—3 sts.
Row 2 Purl.
Row 3 K1, kfb, k1—4 sts
Row 4 Purl.
Row 5 K1, k2tog, k1—3 sts.
Row 6 Purl.
Row 7 K3tog. Secure last st, leaving a tail for sewing.

Assembly
Fold square into triangle (fold at center black dotted line on diagram). Baste stitch body through both thicknesses, left side and right side, to dots. Sew leg seams. Stuff body through mouth opening. Sew mouth seam, leaving an opening in center for tongue.
Pull legs up and tack close to each side of body. Bend to form knees and tack in place. Place a rubber band ½"/1.5cm from bottom of each leg to form feet.
Sew on bobbles, eyelids and tongue, using diagram for placement.
With black yarn, embroider straight st along center of yellow eye.
Sew bead in center of black line. ❀

Eloise the Elephant

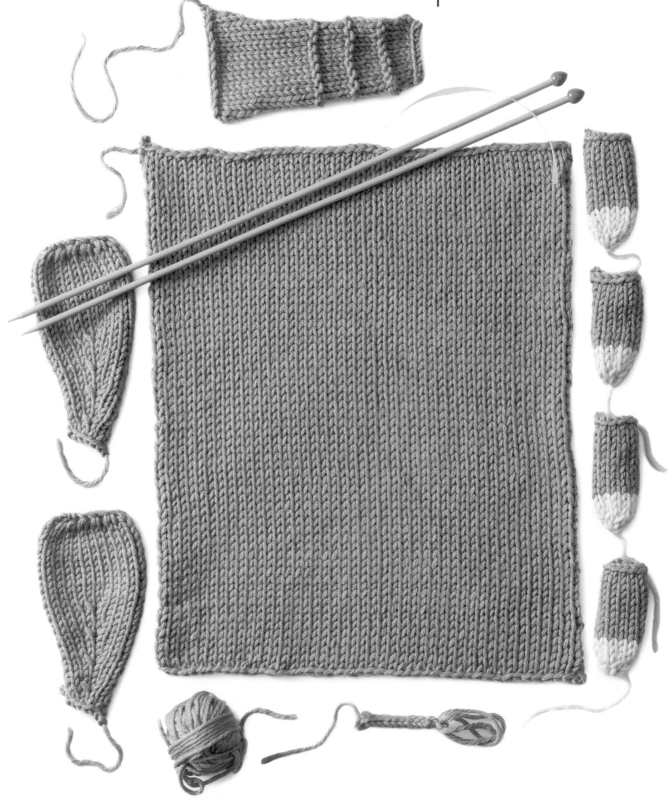

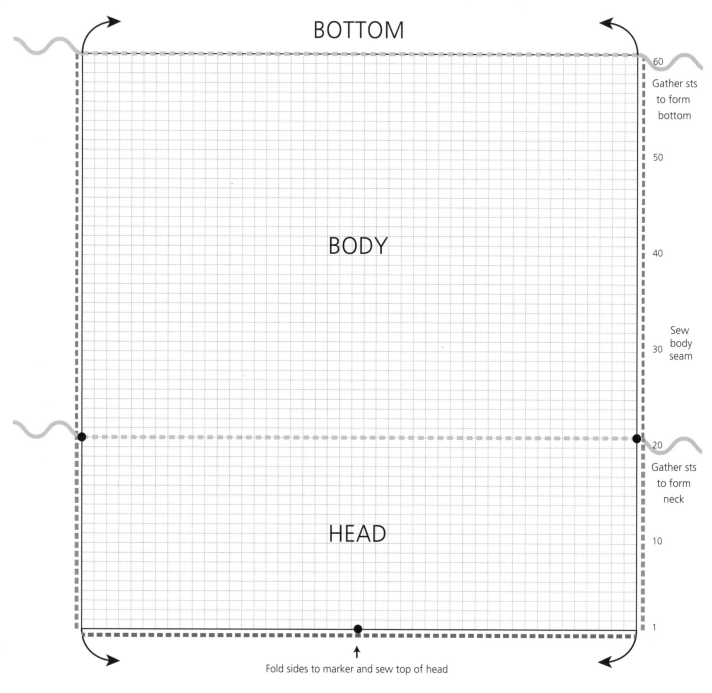

BOTTOM

60

Gather sts
to form
bottom

50

BODY

40

30

Sew
body
seam

20

Gather sts
to form
neck

10

HEAD

1

Fold sides to marker and sew top of head

● = Marker

Eloise will never forget
her favorite trick—
balancing a ball on her trunk.

Materials

- 1 3½oz/100g balls (each approx
210yd/193m) of Berroco Comfort (nylon/
acrylic) each in #9719 Grey (A), #9710 Ballet
Pink (B) and #9773 Lagoon (C) **4**
- Small amount of black yarn for embroidery
- One pair size 7 (4.5mm) needles,
OR SIZE TO OBTAIN GAUGE
- Two size 7 (4.5mm) double-pointed
needles (dpn) for tail only
- Small snap
- Small length pink ribbon ¼"/6mm wide
- Stitch markers
- Polyster stuffing
- Tapestry needle

Gauge

18 sts and 24 rows to 4"/10cm over St st using size 7 (4.5mm) needles.
TAKE TIME TO CHECK GAUGE.

Square

(approx 10"/25.5cm square)
With A, cast on 45 sts.
Work in St st (k on RS, p on WS) for 60 rows. Bind off.

Trunk

With A, cast on 13 sts. Beg with a purl row, work in St st for 14 rows.
*Row 15 (WS) Knit.
Row 16 K1, ssk, k to last 3 sts, k2tog, k1—2 sts dec'd.
Row 17 Purl.
Rows 18 and 20 Knit.
Row 19 Purl.
Rows 20–31 Rep rows 15–20 twice. Bind off rem 7 sts. Sew trunk seam and stuff lightly.

Ears (make 2)

With A, cast on 7 sts.
Row 1 (RS) K into front and back of every st—14 sts.
Rows 2–12 Beg with a purl row, work in St st.
Row 13 (RS) K5, ssk, k2tog, k5—12 sts.
Rows 14–16 Work even in St st.
Rep rows 13–16, working 1 less st before and after decs every dec row until 6 sts remain. Bind off.

Legs (make 4)

With B, cast on 13 sts. Work 4 rows in St st. Cut B and change to A. Work 10 rows in St st. Bind off. Sew leg seams and stuff.

Tail

With dpn and B, cast on 3 sts.
*Row 1 (RS) Knit. Do *not* turn work. Slide the sts back to the opposite end of needle to work next row from RS. Pull yarn tightly from the end of the row. Rep from * for approx 1½"/4cm.
Last row SK2P. Make loop st in last st as foll: Insert RH needle into st as if to knit it. Wind yarn over RH needle and around index finger of left hand 3 times, then over RH needle point once more. Draw all loops

through st on LH needle, then slip loops to LH needle. Insert RH needle through back of these loops and original st and knit them together through back loops. Secure last st. Cut the loops.

Skirt

With C, cast on 102 sts.
Rows 1 and 2 Knit.
Rows 3–6 Beg with a knit row, work in St st.
Rows 7 and 8 With B and beg with a knit row, work in St st. Cut B.
Row 9 With C, knit.
Row 10 [P2tog] 51 times—51 sts.
Rows 11 and 13 *K1, p1; rep from *, end k1.
Rows 12 and 14 *P1, k1; rep from *, end p1.
Bind off. Sew snap at top of waistband.

Bow

With C, cast on 9 sts.
Row 1 (RS) *K1, p1; rep from *, end k1.
Row 2 P1, *k1, p1; rep from * to end.
Rows 3–14 Rep rows 1 and 2 six more times. Bind off. With a length of C, gather and wrap around the center and secure ends.

· ·

Assembly

Lay square on a flat surface.
With a long length of yarn, sew running sts along bound-off edge to mark the bottom, leaving a long length at both ends. Place marker on center stitch of cast-on edge. Count up 20 rows from cast-on edge on both sides, place markers, and sew running sts through sts along this row to mark the neck, leaving a long length at both ends.

Bottom

Pull both ends of the running-st yarn that marked the bottom, gathering the fabric until the outer edges meet at the center, then tie the ends in a double knot tightly.

Head

Pull both ends of the running-st yarn that marked the neck, gathering to shape the head (see photo).
Fold head so sides meet at center marker on cast-on edge. Stuff head, then sew top of head, gathering sts slightly. Sew back of head.

Body

Stuff the remainder of the body firmly. Pin the remaining two sides together and sew the body seam.

Finishing Details

Sew ears to top of head and trunk to center of face. Sew arms and legs in place (see photo). Sew tail to center of back. With black yarn, embroider duplicate stitch for eyes. With C, embroider stem under trunk for mouth. Attach bow to top of head. Wrap skirt around body and snap to close in place. Sew ribbon on each side of skirt for straps (see photo). ❀

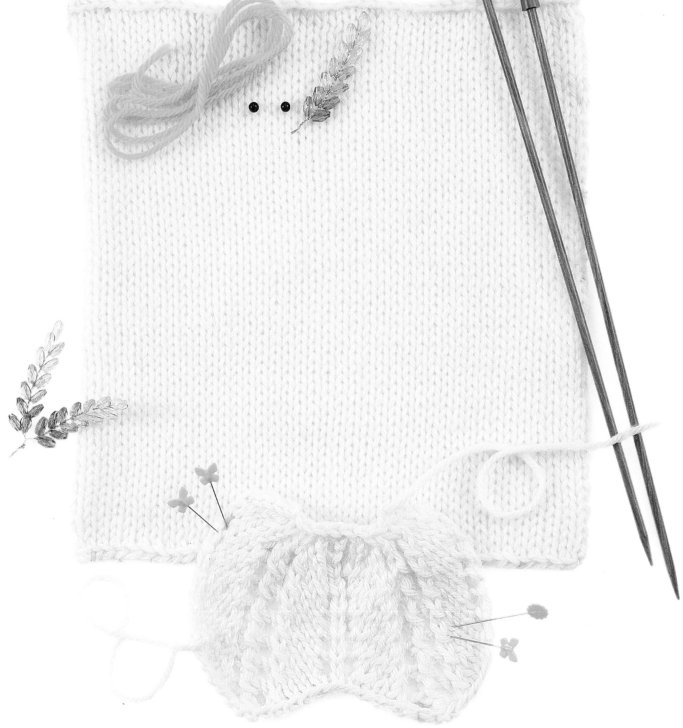

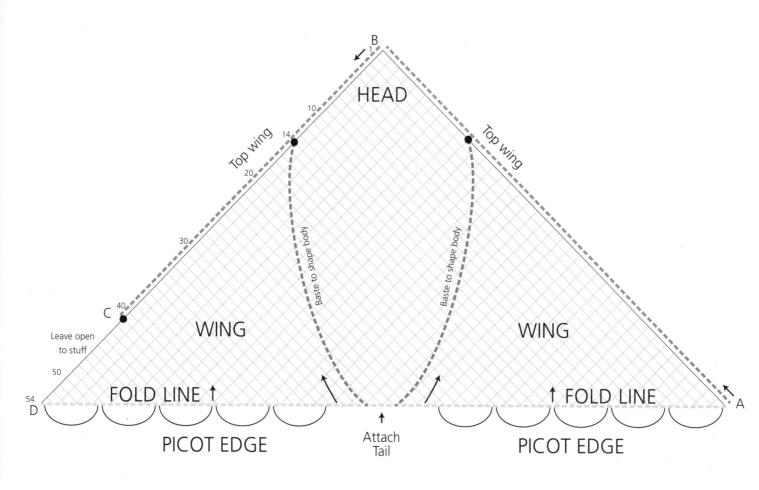

B

1

HEAD

10

14 Top wing

Top wing

20

Baste to shape body

Baste to shape body

30

WING

WING

C 40

Leave open
to stuff

50

FOLD LINE ↑

↑ FOLD LINE

54

D

A

PICOT EDGE

Attach
Tail

PICOT EDGE

Stella loves spreading her
message of peace to all!
Imagine her perched
on your holiday wreath.

Materials

- 1 3½oz/100g skeins (each approx
220yd/200m) of Cascade Yarns Cascade
220 (Peruvian wool) in #8505 White (4)
- Small amount of orange for beak
- One pair each sizes 5 and 8
(3.75 and 5mm) needles,
OR SIZE TO OBTAIN GAUGE
- Two small black beads for eyes
- Stitch markers
- Polyester stuffing
- Tapestry needle

Gauge

18 sts and 24 rows to 4"/10cm over St st using larger needles.
TAKE TIME TO CHECK GAUGE.

Square

(approx 9"/23cm square)
With larger needles, cast on 40 sts.
Work in St st (k on RS, p on WS) for 54 rows.
Bind off.

Tail

With larger needles, cast on 29 sts.
Row 1 and all WS rows Purl.
Rows 2, 4, 6, 8, 10 and 12 K1, *yo, k3, SKP, yo, SK2P, yo, k2tog, k3, yo, k1; rep from * to end
Row 14 (RS) K2tog across row while binding off. Secure last st.
Fold WS together in half and sew tog.

Beak

With smaller needles and orange yarn, cast on 10 sts.
Row 1 (RS) K2tog, k1, k2tog, k2tog, k1, k2tog—6 sts.
Row 2 Purl.
Row 3 [K2tog] 3 times—3 sts.
Row 4 P3tog. Secure last st, leaving a tail for sewing.
Fold in half lengthwise and sew together.

. . . .

Assembly

Lay square on a flat surface.
Fold square into triangle with right sides together, head at top.
With yarn and tapestry needle, sew through both thicknesses along blue dotted line from A to B to C, leaving a 2"/5cm opening from C to D.
Turn inside out to right side.
Baste stitch to shape right side of body (red dotted line on the right) to keep stuffing from right wing area.
Stuff through the 2"/5cm opening to fill head and body. **Note** If felting the dove, use a little less stuffing.
Baste stitch left side of body (red dotted lines on the left), making sure stuffing is contained in body area only and kept from the left wing area.

Sew 2"/5cm opening closed.
Pull top of wings toward back of head and tack in place.
Fold wings toward body and tack in place at tail on each side.

Finishing Details

Sew on beak, sew on beads for eyes (if felting the dove, sew on eyes after felting).

Picot Edge

With RS facing and smaller needle, pick up and k 13 sts along bottom of each wing edge, starting from body to wing tip. Bind off 2 sts, *sl rem st from RH to LH needle. Cast on 3 sts, then bind off 5 sts; rep from * to end. Secure last st.
Sew tail to body between wings.

Felting (optional)

Place finished dove into a mesh laundry bag. Set the machine on the hot wash/cold rinse cycle, set the water level as low as possible. Wash with a few other colorfast items, such as white towels, for agitation and use a small amount of liquid soap.
Reshape dove and let dry.
Sew on beads for eyes. ✿

Grayson the Squirrel

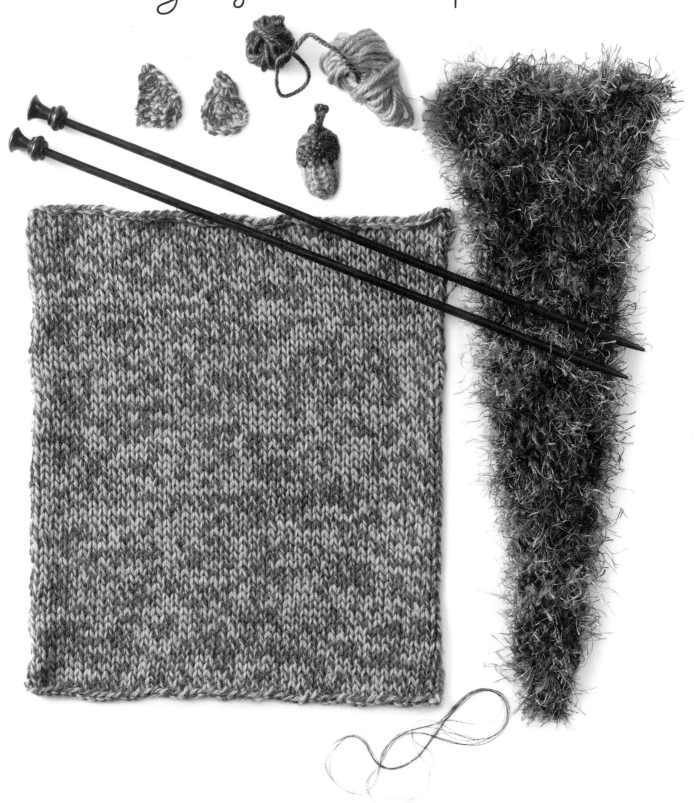

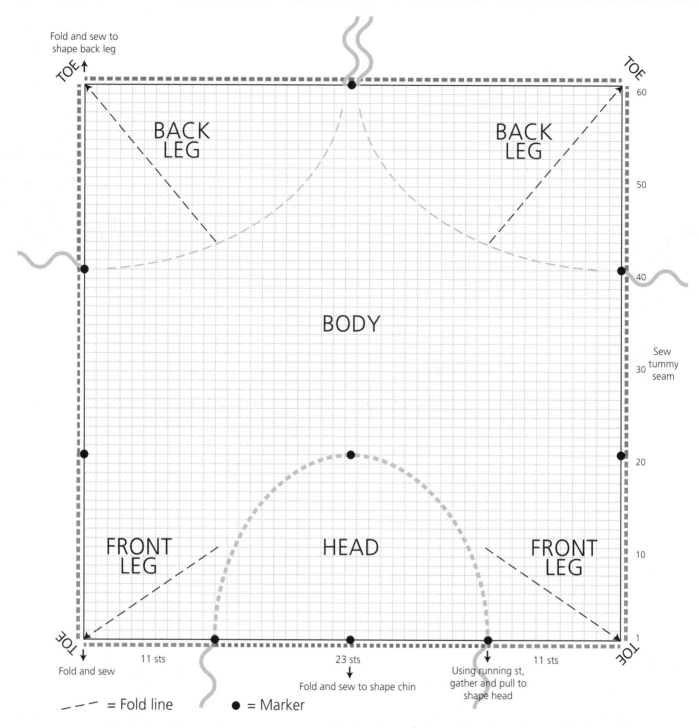

Fold and sew to shape back leg

TOE

BACK LEG

BACK LEG

TOE

60

50

40

BODY

Sew tummy seam

30

FRONT LEG

HEAD

FRONT LEG

20

10

1

TOE

TOE

11 sts

Fold and sew

23 sts

↓

Fold and sew to shape chin

Using running st, gather and pull to shape head

11 sts

– – – = Fold line   ● = Marker

Squirrels are nuts about nuts, and Grayson is no exception.
He's stocking up for winter...
and his nutty holiday parties.

Materials

- 1 3½oz/100g skein (each approx 170yd/156m) of Lion Brand Yarn Vanna's Choice (acrylic) in #405 Silver Heather (A) (4)
- 1 1¾oz/50g skein (each approx 64yd/58m) of Lion Brand Yarn Fun Fur (polyester) in #204 Lava (B) (5)

- One pair size 8 (5mm) needles, OR SIZE TO OBTAIN GAUGE
- Small amount of black yarn to embroider face and paws
- Small amount of black sewing thread for whiskers
- Stitch markers and tapestry needle
- Polyester stuffing

Gauge
16 sts and 22 rows to 4"/10cm over St st and Vanna's Choice using size 8 (5mm) needles. TAKE TIME TO CHECK GAUGE.

Square
(approx 11"/28cm square)
With A, cast on 45 sts.
Work in St st (k on RS, p on WS) for 60 rows. Bind off.

Ears (make 2)
With A, cast on 7 sts. Work in St st for 4 rows.
Row 5 (RS) K2, SK2P, k2—5 sts.
Row 6 Purl.
Row 7 K1, SK2P, k1—3 sts.
Row 8 Sl 1, p2tog, psso.
Secure last st.

Tail
With 1 strand A and B held tog, cast on 20 sts. Work in St st for 36 rows.
Inc 1 st each side of next row, then every other row once more—24 sts.
Dec 1 st each side every other row twice—20 sts.
Dec 1 st each side every 4ᵗʰ row 9 times—2 sts.
P2tog.
Secure last st.

· ·

Assembly
Lay square on a flat surface.
Mark the center 23 sts along cast-on edge. Place marker on center st on cast-on row, then measure up 20 rows from center st and place another marker. Cut a piece of yarn approx 25"/63.5cm long and sew running sts to outline the head, following the diagram for placement and leaving a long length at both ends.
Place markers along each side edge at 20 rows from cast-on and bound-off edges to mark one half of each leg. Mark the center st along bound-off edge to mark other half of each back leg.
Cut a piece of yarn approx 25"/63.5cm long and sew running sts to outline the back legs only, following the diagram for placement and leaving a long length at both ends.

Head
Pull both ends of the running-st yarn that marked the head, gathering the fabric until the outer edges meet at the center, then tie the ends in a double knot tightly. Stuff the head firmly. Fold head in half, pin and sew cast-on sts tog for chin seam.

Front Legs
Fold one front leg so that side edges (blue dotted lines) meet and form a point at the outer edge (toe), easing the longer side into the shorter side, and pin the edges together. Sew the side edges together. Fold and sew the other front leg in same way. Stuff the legs firmly.

Back Legs
Pull both ends of the running-st yarn that marked the legs, gathering the fabric slightly until the outer edges meet at the center, then tie the ends in a double knot tightly. Sew and stuff same as front legs.

Tummy
Stuff the remainder of the body firmly. Pin the remaining two sides together and sew the tummy seam.

Tail
Gather cast-on sts tog. Fold first 36 rows of tail so that sides edges meet and sew back seam. Sew the cast-on edge of tail to butt between the legs.

Finishing Details
Sew ears to head, leaving approx 1½"/4cm between the ears (use photo as a guide). With black yarn, embroider French knots for eyes, embroider nose with satin st in center of face, then embroider mouth with straight sts. With black sewing thread, embroider straight sts for whiskers.

Acorn
Materials
- Small amounts of fingering or DK weight yarn in brown and gold for acorn
- One pair size 2 (2.75mm) needles
- Small amount of polyester stuffing
- Tapestry needle

Base
With gold yarn, cast on 4 sts, leaving long tail for seaming.
Row 1 (RS) Kfb in each st—8 sts.
Rows 2, 4 and 6 Purl.
Rows 3 and 5 Knit.
Cut gold yarn.

Top
Change to brown yarn.
Row 7 K1, [kfb] 6 times, k1—14 sts.
Rows 8–11 Knit.
Row 12 [K2tog] 7 times—8 sts.
Row 13 [K2tog] 4 times—4 sts.
Row 14 K4tog—1 st.
Work stem as foll: cast on 4 sts, bind off 5 sts. Secure last st.

Finishing
Cut yarn. With tapestry needle, thread tail through rem sts on needle. Gather and fasten securely, but do *not* cut. Stuff lightly. Gather cast-on edge with cast-on tail, sew seam, fasten off. ✿

Theo the Triceratops

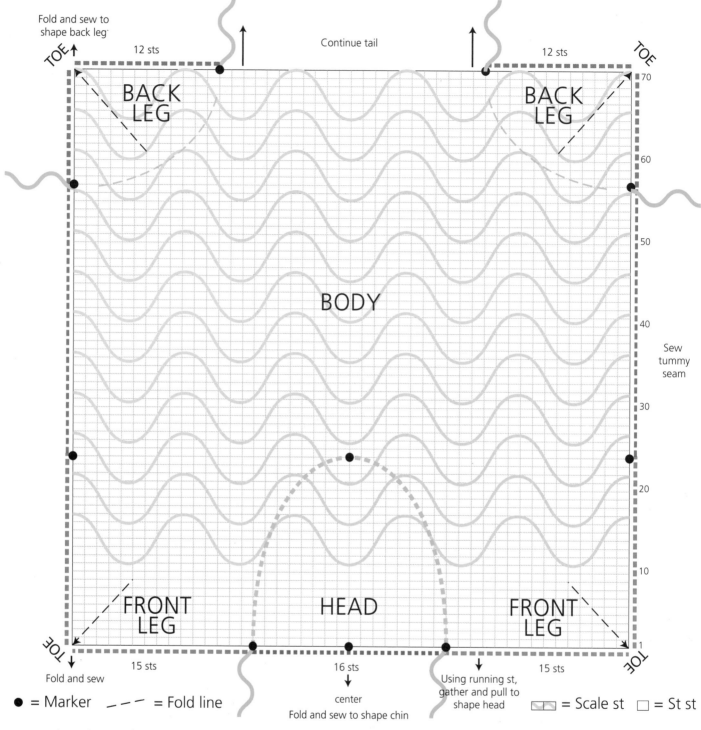

Fold and sew to shape back leg

TOE ↑   12 sts   Continue tail   12 sts   TOE

BACK LEG   BACK LEG

70

60

BODY

50

40

Sew tummy seam

30

FRONT LEG   HEAD   FRONT LEG

20

10

TOE ↓   15 sts   16 sts   15 sts   TOE ↓

Fold and sew

center
Fold and sew to shape chin

Using running st, gather and pull to shape head

● = Marker   _ _ _ = Fold line   🟦 = Scale st   ☐ = St st

Don't let Theo's flashy frill fool you. He's the sweetest dinosaur you'll ever meet.

Materials
- 1 1¾oz/50g skein (each approx 125yd/112m) of Noro Yarn/KFI Hanabatake (wool/silk/mohair) in #6 Brown/Wine/Pink/Green (4)
- One pair size 7 (4.5mm) needles, OR SIZE TO OBTAIN GAUGE
- 2 beads for eyes
- Stitch markers
- Polyester stuffing
- Tapestry needle

Gauge

18 sts and 30 rows to 4"/10cm over scale st pat using size 7 (4.5mm) needles.
TAKE TIME TO CHECK GAUGE

Scale Stitch Pattern

(over a multiple of 8 sts plus 6)
Row 1 (RS) K6, *p2, k6; rep from * to end.
Row 2 K1, *p4, k4; rep from *, end p4, k1.
Row 3 P2, *k2, p2; rep from * to end.
Row 4 P1, *k4, p4; rep from *, end k4, p1.
Row 5 K2, *p2, k6; rep from *, end p2, k2.
Row 6 P6, *k2, p6; rep from * to end.
Row 7 P1, *k4, p4; rep from *, end k4, p1.
Row 8 K2, *p2, k2; rep from * to end.
Row 9 K1, *p4, k4; rep from *, end p4, k1.
Row 10 P2, *k2, p6; rep from *, end k2, p2.
Rep rows 1–10 for scale st pat.

Square

(approx 10"/25.5cm square)
Cast on 46 sts.
Work in St st (k on RS, p on WS) for 10 rows.
Rep rows 1–10 of scale st pat 10 times (60 rows in total).
Next row (RS) Bind off 12 sts, k until there are 22 sts from bind off for tail, join a short length of yarn and bind off rem 12 sts.

Tail

Cont on 22 sts for tail as foll: Beg with a purl row, work in St st for 5 rows more.
Row 1 (RS) K9, ssk, k2tog, k9—20 sts.
Row 2 Purl.
Row 3 Knit.
Row 4 Purl.
Rep rows 1–4, working 1 less st at beg and end of the dec row 1, until 4 sts rem.
Next row (WS) Purl.
Next row Ssk, k2tog.
Next row P2tog. Secure last st, leaving a 16"/40.5cm tail for sewing.

Frill

Cast on 17 sts, leaving a long tail for sewing.
Row 1 (RS) K1, *p1, k1; rep from * to end.
Row 2 P1, *k1, p1; rep from * to end
Row 3 K1, *p1, M1p, k1; rep from * to end—25 sts.
Row 4 P1, *k2, p1; rep from * to end.
Row 5 K1, *p2, M1p, k1; rep from * to end—33 sts.

Row 6 P1, *k3, p1; rep from * to end
Row 7 K1, *p3, M1p, k1; rep from * to end—41 sts.
Row 8 P1, *k4, p1; rep from * to end.
Row 9 K1, *p4, M1p, k1; rep from * to end—49 sts.
Row 10 P1, *k5, p1; rep from * to end.
Bind off 6 sts at beg of next 7 rows, keeping in pattern. Bind off rem 7 sts.

Head Horns (make 2)

Cast on 5 sts.
Rows 1–6 Beg with a knit row, work in St st.
Row 7 (RS) K1, SK2P, k1—3 sts.
Row 8 Purl.
Row 9 SK2P. Secure last st. Work in ends.

Nose Horn

Work same as head horns, but work 2 rows (instead of 6) in St st before working dec row 7.

. . . .

Assembly

Lay square on a flat surface.
Mark the center 16 along cast-on edge.
Mark the center st and count up 23 rows from center st and place another marker.
Cut a piece of yarn approx 25"/63.5cm long and sew running sts to outline the head, following the diagram for placement and leaving a long length at both ends.
Place markers along each side edge at 23 rows from cast-on edge to mark one half of each front leg. Place markers along each side edge at 14 rows from bound-off edge to mark one half of each back leg. Cut a piece of yarn approx 25"/63.5cm long and sew running sts to outline the back legs only, following the diagram for placement and leaving a long length at both ends.

Head

Pull both ends of the running-st yarn that marked the head, gathering the fabric until the outer edges meet at the center, then tie the ends in a double knot tightly. Stuff the head firmly. Fold head in half, pin and sew cast-on sts tog for chin seam.

Front Legs

Fold one front leg so that side edges (blue dotted lines) meet and form a point at the

outer edge (toe), easing the longer side into the shorter side, and pin the edges together. Sew the side edges together. Fold and sew the other front leg in same way. Stuff the legs firmly.

Back Legs

Pull both ends of the running-st yarn that marked the back legs, gathering slightly, then tie the ends in a double knot tightly. Fold one back leg so that side edges (green dotted lines) meet and form a point at the outer edge (toe), easing the longer side into the shorter side, and pin the edges together. Sew the side edges together. Gather, fold and sew the other back leg in same way. Stuff the legs firmly.

Tail and Tummy

Sew tail seam and stuff firmly.
Stuff the remainder of the body firmly.
Pin the remaining two sides together and sew the tummy seam.

Finishing Details

Sew head horns to center back of head, approx ¼"/1cm apart.
Sew frill to back of head at gather.
Sew nose horn to top of nose.
Embroider mouth with straight sts.
Sew on beads for eyes.
(Use photo as a guide). ✾

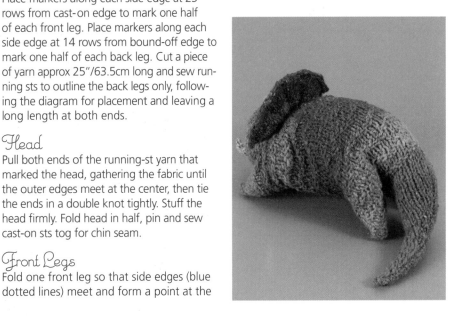

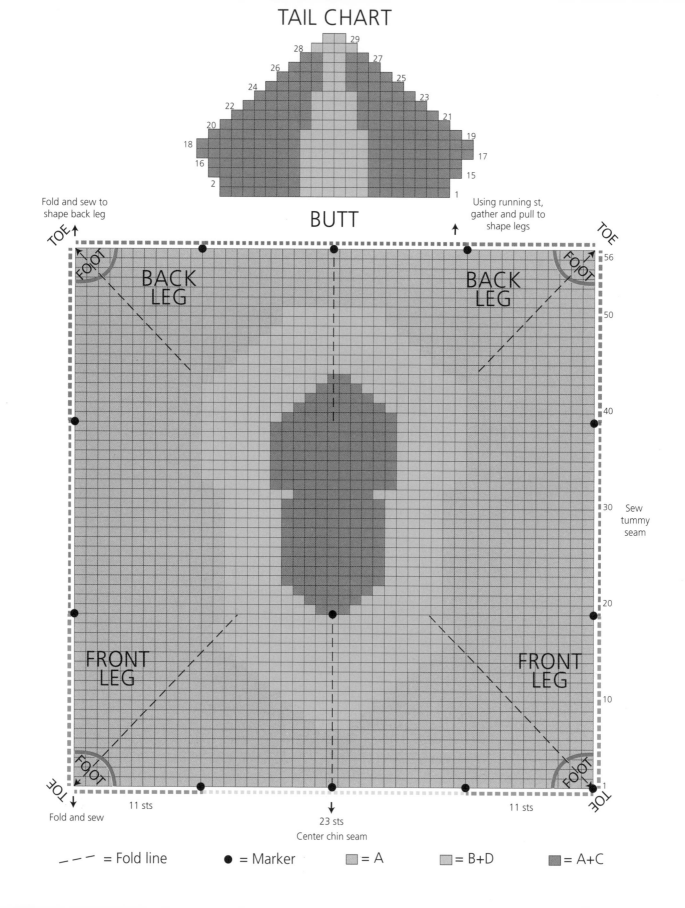

TAIL CHART

29
28
26
27
24
25
22
23
20
21
18
19
16
17
15
2
1

BUTT

Fold and sew to shape back leg

Using running st, gather and pull to shape legs

TOE

TOE

FOOT

BACK LEG

BACK LEG

FOOT

56

50

40

40

Sew tummy seam

30

20

20

FRONT LEG

FRONT LEG

FOOT

FOOT

10

TOE

TOE

1

11 sts

11 sts

Fold and sew

23 sts
Center chin seam

- - - = Fold line   ● = Marker   ☐ = A   ☐ = B+D   ☐ = A+C

Sebastian lives in a lovely flower patch on a sunny hill. He's the sweetest-smelling skunk you'll ever meet.

Materials
- 1 3½oz/100g skein (each approx 170yd/156m) of Lion Brand Yarn Vanna's Choice (acrylic) each in #153 Black (A) and #100 White (B) (4)
- 1 1¾oz/50g skein (each approx 64yd/58m) of Lion Brand Yarn Fun Fur (polyester) each in #153 Black (C) and #100 White (D) (5)
- One pair size 8 (5mm) needles, OR SIZE TO OBTAIN GAUGE
- Small amount of pink yarn for face embroidery
- 2 blue beads for eyes
- Stitch markers
- Polyester stuffing
- Tapestry needle

Gauge
16 sts and 22 rows to 4"/10cm over St st and 1 strand Vanna's Choice using size 8 (5mm) needles.
TAKE TIME TO CHECK GAUGE.

Note
When working chart, use separate lengths (butterflies) of yarn for each block of color and when changing colors, twist yarns on WS to prevent holes in work.

Square
(approx 11"/28cm square)
Cast on 45 sts.
Work in St st (k on RS, p on WS) and follow chart for 56 rows. Bind off.

Ears (make 2)
With A, cast on 7 sts.
Knit 1 row, pass all sts over first st and off needle, one at a time.
Pull yarn through last st to secure.

Tail
With A, cast on 7 sts; with 1 strand B and D cast on 6 sts, with a length or butterfly of A, cast on 7 sts—20 sts in total. Work in St st and Tail Chart as foll:
Row 1 (RS) K7 A, k6 B and D, k7 A.
Row 2 (WS) P7 A, p6 B and D, p7 A.
Rows 3–14 Rep rows 1 and 2 five times.
Row 15 (RS) With A, kfb, k to center 6 sts; k6 B and D; with A, k to last st, kfb—2 sts inc'd. Cont working increases and decreases as shown on chart, through row 29. Bind off rem 2 sts.

· ·

Assembly
Mark the center 23 sts along cast-on edge. Mark the center st, measure up 18 rows from center st and place another marker. Place markers along each side edge at 18 rows from cast-on and bound-off edges to mark one half of each leg.

Head
Fold head in half and sew cast-on sts tog for chin seam. Stuff the head firmly, shaping stuffing with tapestry needle if necessary.

Front Legs
Fold one front leg so that side edges (blue dotted lines) meet and form a point at the outer edge (toe), easing the longer side into the shorter side, and pin the edges together. Sew the side edges together, leaving approx ¼"/1cm unsewn at tip of toe. Fold and sew the other front leg in same way. Stuff the legs firmly. Wrap a length of yarn about 3 times around the center of the toe at the base where the toe was left unsewn so that the toes curl and form the paws.

Back Legs
Work same as front legs.

Butt
Fold in half at center and sew bound-off edges tog.

Tummy
Stuff the remainder of the body firmly. Pin rem two sides tog and sew tummy seam.

Tail
Fold first 14 rows of tail so that sides edges meet and sew back seam. Stuff lightly and stitch to hold the stuffing in place.
Sew tail approx ¼"/1cm above butt point.

Finishing Details
Sew ears to head just below the white stripe and approx 1"/2.5cm apart.
With B, make 2 duplicate sts for eyes. Sew on beads in center of duplicate sts. With pink yarn, embroider nose with satin st in center of face, then with B embroider face stripe with stem st. ❁

Socrates the Owl

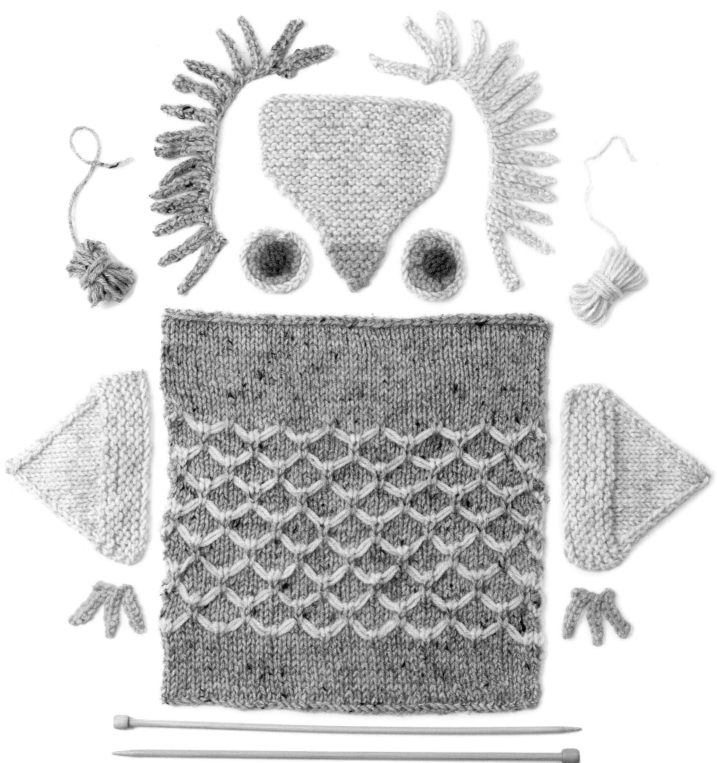

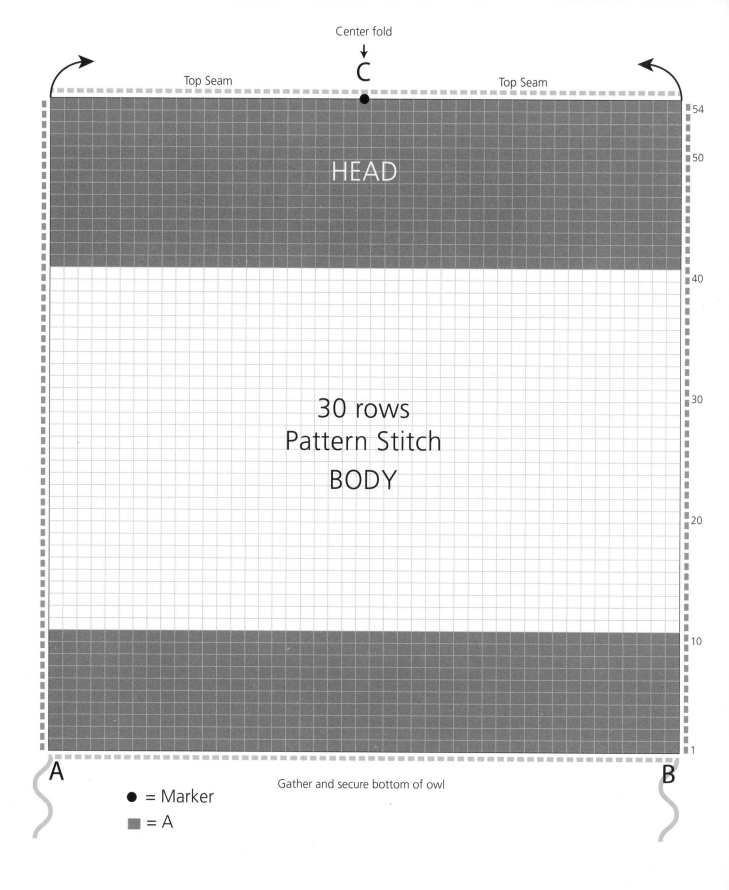

Center fold

C

Top Seam   Top Seam

HEAD

54

50

40

30 rows
Pattern Stitch
BODY

30

20

10

1

A   Gather and secure bottom of owl   B

● = Marker

▨ = A

All the animals
come to this wise old owl
for knitting advice.
You can too!

Materials
- 1 3oz/85g ball (each approx 145yd/133m) of Lion Brand Vanna's Choice (acrylic/rayon) each in #401 Light Grey Tweed (A) and #305 Linen and Cream Heather (B) 🏷️4
- Small amount in gold and rust
- One pair size 9 (5.5mm) needles, OR SIZE TO OBTAIN GAUGE
- Stitch markers
- Polyester stuffing
- Tapestry needle

Gauge
17 sts and 20 rows to 4"/10cm over St st using size 8 (5mm) needles.
TAKE TIME TO CHECK GAUGE.

Note
When working in pattern st, it is important to keep the color B strands loose as they are carried across the front of the fabric.

Pattern Stitch
(over a multiple of 6 sts plus 3)
Row 1 (RS) With B, k2, *sl 5 wyif; k1; rep from * to last st, k1.
Row 2 With B, p2, *sl 5 wyib; p1; rep from * to last st, p1.
Row 3 With A, knit.
Row 4 With A, purl.
Row 5 With A, k4, *insert needle under the loose color B strands and k next st, catching both strands behind st as it is knitted, k5; rep from *, end last rep k4.
Row 6 With A, purl.
Row 7 With B, k1, sl 3 wyif, *k1, sl 5 wyif; rep from *, end k1, sl 3 wyif, k1.
Row 8 With B, p1, sl 3 wyib, *p1, sl 5 wyib; rep from * end p1, sl 3 wyib, p1.
Rows 9 and 10 With A, rep rows 3 and 4.
Row 11 With A, k1, *insert needle under the loose color B strands and k next st, k5;

rep from *, end last rep k1.
Row 12 With A, purl.
Rep rows 1–12 for pattern stitch.

Square
(approx 10"/25.5cm square)
With A, cast on 45 sts and work in St st (k on RS, p on WS) for 10 rows.
Rep rows 1–12 of pattern stitch twice, then rep rows 1–6 once more—30 rows total in pat.
With A, work in St st for 14 rows. Bind off.

Horn and Beak
With B, cast on 23 sts. Work garter st (knit every row) for 2"/5cm.
Row 1 (RS) Ssk, k to last 2 sts, k2tog.
Row 2 (WS) Knit.
Rows 3–16 Rep rows 1 and 2 seven more times—7 sts.
Rows 17–20 Knit.
Cut B, join Gold.
Row 21 Rep row 1—5 sts.
Rows 22–24 Knit.
Row 25 Rep row 1—3 sts.
Row 26 Knit.
Row 27 SKP. Secure last st.

Eyes (make 2)
With B, cast on 26 sts. Change to gold. Knit 3 rows. Pass all sts over the 1st and off the needle one st at a time. Form a circle, leaving small opening.

Pupil (make 2)
With brown, make a slipknot.
Row 1 (RS) K into front, back, front and back of st—4 sts.
Rows 2 and 4 Purl.
Row 3 Knit.
Row 5 [K2tog] twice.
Row 6 P2tog. Secure last st.

Wings
With B, cast on 21 sts.
Rows 1–10 Knit.
Row 11 (RS) K1, ssk, k to last 3 sts, k2tog, k1.
Row 12 Purl.
Rows 13–26 Rep rows 11 and 12 seven times—5 sts.
Row 27 K1, SK2P, k1—3 sts.
Row 28 P1, p2tog, psso. Secure last st.

Gather cast-on edge and secure.

Feathers (make 2: 1 in A and 1 in B)
Using single cast on method (see page 142), *cast on 9 sts, bind off 8 sts. Place rem st on LH needle. Rep from * 14 more times. Secure last st.

Talons (make 2)
With gold, work same as feathers, but cast on 7 sts and bind off 6 sts three times.

. . . .

Assembly
Thread tapestry needle and sew running stitches on diagram from point A to point B. Place a marker on center st of bound-off edge. Fold A to B (two blue lines) so that edges meet at the center fold (C on diagram) and sew back seam. Sew cast-on sts for top of head seam. Stuff body, pull gather tightly and secure for bottom. Using photo as guide, assemble as foll:
Sew cast-on edge of horn and beak along top of head, fold and tack beak to front.
Sew eyes in place, attach pupils.
Sew wings to sides of owl.
Sew talons along bottom edge.
Sew B feathers across top head seam.
Sew A feathers ½"/1cm below B feathers. ❀

Ella the Bunny

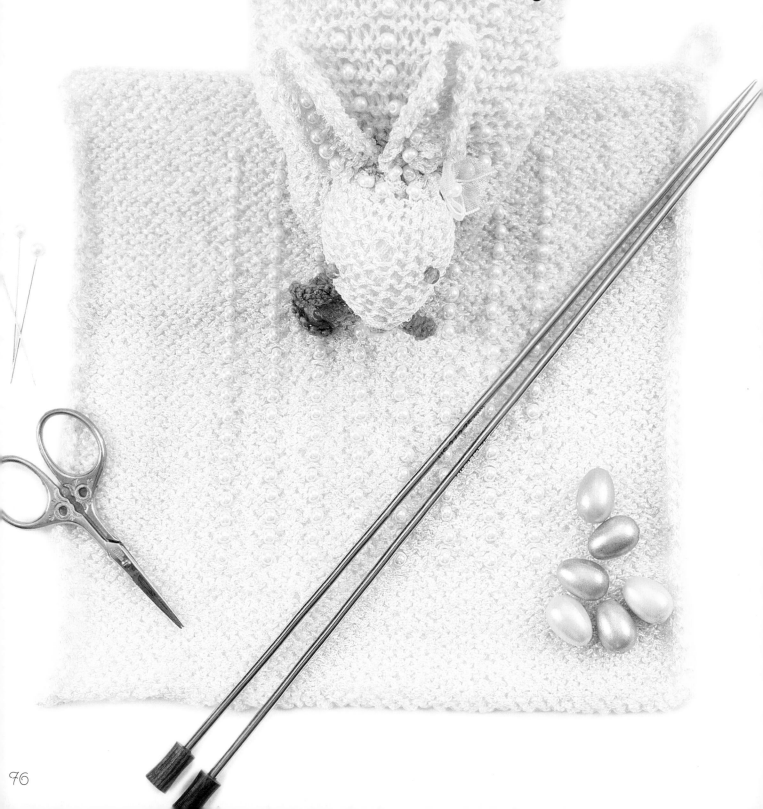

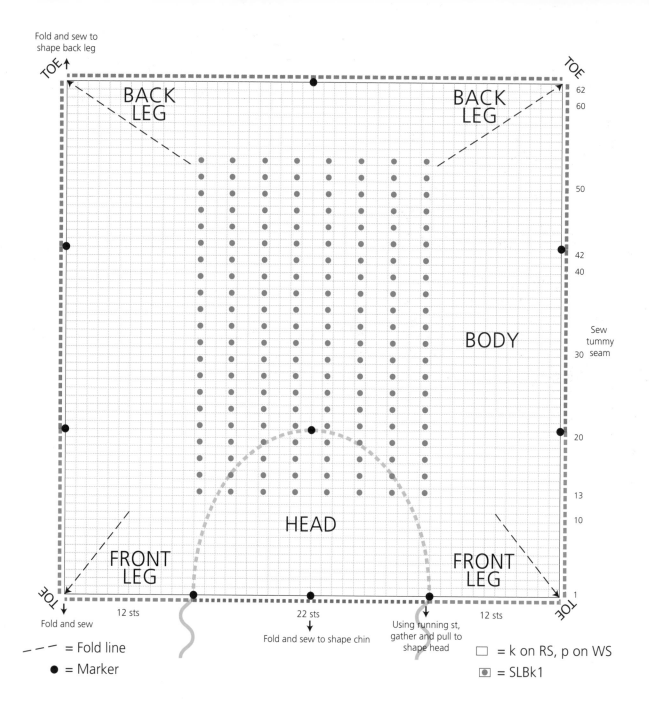

Fold and sew to shape back leg

TOE↑ TOE

BACK LEG   BACK LEG

62
60

BODY

50

Sew tummy seam

42
40

30

20

13
10

HEAD

FRONT LEG   FRONT LEG

1

TOE   TOE

12 sts   22 sts   12 sts

Fold and sew   Fold and sew to shape chin   Using running st, gather and pull to shape head

- - - = Fold line

● = Marker

☐ = k on RS, p on WS

⊙ = SLBk1

Ella, dolled up in beads and a bow, knows carrots are good for eyes. Did you ever see a bunny wearing glasses?

Materials
BUNNY
- 1 .88oz/25g skein (each approx 132yd/120m) of Filatura di Crosa/Tahki•Stacy Charles New Smoking (viscose/polyester) in #7 White (3)
- One pair size 4 (3.5mm) needles OR SIZE TO OBTAIN GAUGE
- 178 Beads iridescent white size 6/0
- 2 small pink beads for eyes

- Small light pink ribbon bow
- Small amount pink yarn for mouth
- Stitch markers
- Polyester stuffing
- Tapestry needle
CARROT
- Small amount orange and green yarn for carrot (Lion Brand Bon Bons used)
- One pair size 0 (2mm) needles

Notes

String beads onto yarn.
Beads are worked on WS rows.

Gauge

24 sts and 32 rows to 4"/10cm over rev St
st using size 4 (3.5mm) needles.
TAKE TIME TO CHECK GAUGE.

Stitch Glossary

SLBk1 Slip bead to back of next stitch and
knit that stitch.
SLBp1 Slip bead to back of next stitch and
purl that stitch.

Square

(approx 7½"/19cm square)
Cast on 46 sts.
Rows 1–12 Beg with a knit (WS) row, work
in rev St st (p on RS, k on WS) for 12 rows.
Beg Bead Pattern
Row 13 (WS) K12, place marker (pm),
[SLBk1, p2] 7 times, SLBk1, pm, k12.
Row 14 (RS) Purl all sts.
Rows 15–54 Rep last 2 rows 20 times.
Rows 55–62 Work in rev St st. Bind off.

Ears (make 2)

Cast on 7 sts.
Row 1 (WS) Knit.
Row 2 (RS) Purl.
Row 3 K3, SLBk1, k3.
Row 4 Purl.
Rows 5–12 Rep last 2 rows 4 times—5
beads in total.
Row 13 Ssk, k3, k2tog—5 sts.
Row 14 Purl.
Rows 15 Ssk, k1, k2tog—3 sts.
Row 16 Slip 1, p2tog, psso, secure last st.

Tail

Make a slipknot. K into the front, back,
front, back and front of st—5 sts.
Row 1 (RS) Purl.
Rows 2 and 4 (WS) SLBk1, k1, SLBk1, k1, SLBk1.
Rows 3 and 5 Purl.
Row 6 Ssk, k1, k2tog—3 sts.
Row 7 SLBp1, p2tog, psso, secure last st.

Assembly

Lay square on a flat surface. Mark the center 22 sts along cast-on edge. Mark center
st on cast-on edge, measure up 20 rows
from center st and place another marker.
Cut a piece of yarn approx 25"/63.5cm long
and sew running sts to outline the head,
following the diagram for placement and
leaving a long length at both ends.
Place markers along each side edge at 20
rows from cast-on and bound-off edges to
mark one half of each leg. Mark the center
st along bound-off edge to mark other half
of each back leg.

Head

Pull both ends of the running st yarn that
marked the head, gathering the fabric until
the outer edges meet at the center, then
tie the ends in a double knot tightly. Stuff
the head firmly. Fold head in half, pin and
sew cast-on sts tog for chin seam.

Front Legs

Fold one front leg so that side edges (blue
dotted lines) meet and form a point at the
outer edge (toe), easing the longer side
into the shorter side, and pin the edges
together. Sew the side edges together. Fold
and sew the other front leg in same way.
Stuff the legs firmly.

Back Legs

Fold one back leg so that side edges (green
dotted lines) meet at the center marked st
and form a point at the outer edge (toe),
easing the longer side into the shorter side,
and pin the edges together. Sew the side
edges together. Fold and sew the other
back leg in same way. Stuff the legs firmly.

Tummy

Stuff the remainder of the body firmly.
Pin the remaining two sides together and
sew the tummy seam.

Finishing Details

Sew ears to center back of head, next to
each other (use photo as a guide).
Sew tail to top of butt.
Sew on beads for eyes. With pink yarn,
embroider nose with satin st in center of
face, then embroider mouth with straight sts.
Sew light pink bow at one side of neck,
sew a bead in center of bow.

Carrot

With orange, cast on 5 sts.
Row 1 (RS) Kfb in each st—10 sts.
Rows 2, 4 and 6 Purl.
Rows 3 and 5 Knit.
Rows 7, 9 and 11 K3, k2tog, k to end—7 sts
at end of row 11.
Rows 8, 10 and 12 Purl.
Row 13 K2, k3tog, k2—5 sts.
Rows 14 and 16 Purl.
Row 15 K1, SKP, k1—3 sts.
Row 17 SKP.
Gather carrot top, pull tightly and secure,
sew seam.

Leaves

With green, cast on 6 sts. Bind off 5 sts.
Slip last st to LH needle, cast on 6 sts, bind
off 7 sts. Sew to top of carrot. ✿

Chloe & Carrie the Polar Bears

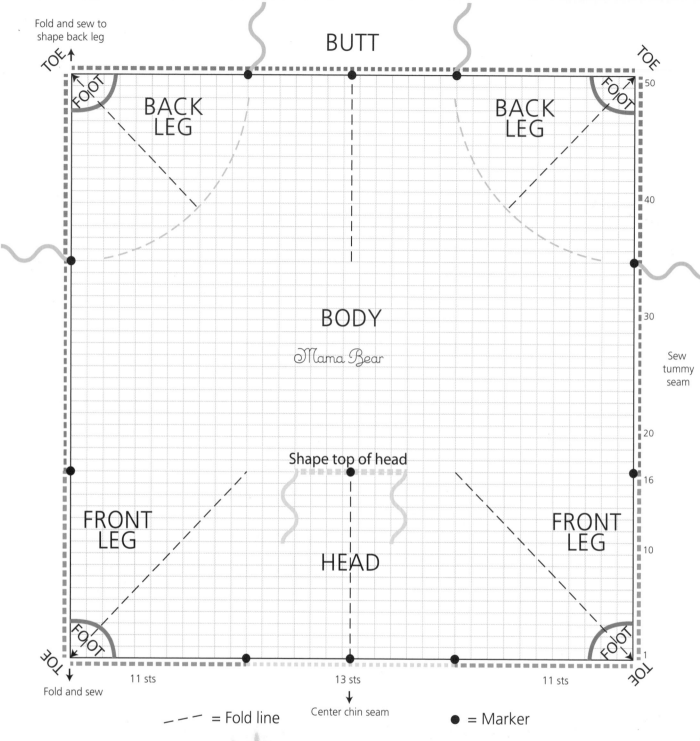

Fold and sew to shape back leg

TOE

FOOT

BUTT

BACK LEG

BACK LEG

TOE

FOOT

50

40

30

BODY

Mama Bear

Sew tummy seam

20

Shape top of head

16

FRONT LEG

FRONT LEG

10

HEAD

FOOT

TOE

FOOT

TOE

Fold and sew

11 sts

13 sts

11 sts

1

Center chin seam

- - - = Fold line   ● = Marker

Carrie bears a remarkable resemblance to her mother, Chloe. They love to cuddle and play on the ice together.

Materials
- 1 1¾oz/50g skein (each approx 109yd/100m) of Plymouth Yarn Arequipa Boucle (baby alpaca/nylon) in #100 Ecru (5)
- One pair size 10 (6mm) needles, OR SIZE TO OBTAIN GAUGE
- Small amount of black yarn for face embroidery
- Small amount of a smooth ecru colored yarn for seaming
- 2 blue beads for eyes, 2 extra small beads for baby bear
- Stitch markers
- Polyester stuffing
- Tapestry needle

Gauge

15 sts and 22 rows to 4"/10cm over St st using size 10 (6mm) needles.
TAKE TIME TO CHECK GAUGE.

Square for Mama Bear

(approx 9¼"/22.5cm square)
Cast on 35 sts.
Work in St st (k on RS, p on WS) for 50 rows. Bind off.

Square for Baby Bear

(approx 6¾"/17cm square)
Cast on 25 sts.
Work in St st for 36 rows. Bind off.

Mama Ears (make 2)

Cast on 7 sts.
Knit 1 row, pass all sts over first st and off needle, one at a time. Pull yarn through last st to secure.

Baby Ears (make 2)

Cast on 5 sts. Complete same as Mama Bear.

Mama Tail

Cast on 6 sts. Bind off 6 sts. Secure last st.

Baby Tail

Cast on 4 sts. Bind off 4 sts. Secure last st.

. . . .

Assembly

Note Use smooth yarn for putting bears together. The diagram is drawn to the size of the Mama Bear. Follow instructions for marking Baby Bear as given below.

Lay square on a flat surface.
Mark the center 13 sts (for Mama) or 9 sts (for Baby) along cast-on edge. Place marker on center st on cast-on edge. Measure up 16 rows (for Mama) or 12 rows (for Baby) from center st and place another marker. Sew running sts along center top of head (pink dotted line), leaving a long length at both ends.
Place markers along each side edge at 16 rows (Mama) or 12 rows (Baby) from cast-on and bound-off edges to mark one half of each leg. Cut a piece of yarn approx 25"/63.5cm long and sew running sts to outline the back legs

only, following the diagram for placement and leaving a long length at both ends.

Head

Fold head in half and sew cast-on sts tog for chin seam. Stuff the head firmly. Pull both ends of the running-st yarn that marked the top of the head and gather sts slightly.

Front Legs

Fold one front leg so that side edges (blue dotted lines) meet and form a point at the outer edge (toe), easing the longer side into the shorter side, and pin the edges together. Sew the side edges together, leaving approx ¼"/1cm unsewn at tip of toe. Fold and sew the other front leg in same way. Stuff the legs firmly. Wrap a length a yarn about 3 times around the center of the toe at the base where the toe was left unsewn so that the toes curl and form the paws.

Back Legs

Pull both ends of the running-st yarn that marked the back legs, gathering the fabric until the outer edges meet at the center, then tie the ends in a double knot tightly. Stuff and make paws same as front legs.

Butt

Fold in half at center and sew bound-off edges tog.

Tummy

Stuff the remainder of the body firmly. Pin the rem two sides together and sew the tummy seam.

Finishing Details

Sew ears to head either side of the top gathers (use photo as a guide).
Sew tail to top of butt.
Sew on beads for eyes.
With black yarn, embroider nose with satin st in center of face, then embroider mouth with straight sts. ✿

Rocky the Racoon

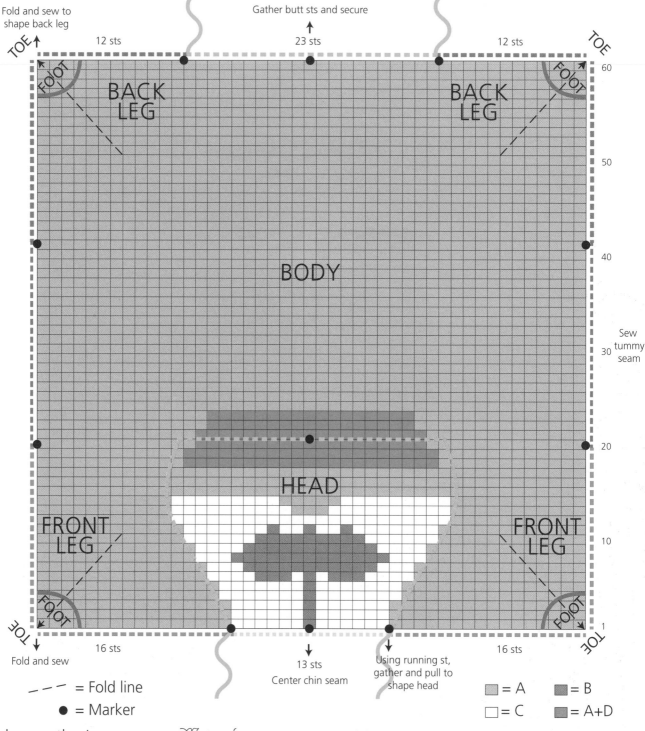

Fold and sew to shape back leg

Gather butt sts and secure

TOE↑

12 sts   23 sts   12 sts

TOE

BACK LEG   BACK LEG

BODY

Sew tummy seam

HEAD

FRONT LEG   FRONT LEG

TOE↓

16 sts   13 sts   16 sts

Fold and sew

Center chin seam

Using running st, gather and pull to shape head

– – – = Fold line

● = Marker

= A   = B

= C   = A+D

Rocky knows the Joneses have the best brunch. How? He's eaten at every trash can in town!

Materials
- 1 3½oz/100g skein (each approx 170yd/156m) of Lion Brand Yarn Vanna's Choice (acrylic) each in #407 Graphite (A), #153 Black (B) and #305 Pearl Mist (C) (4)
- 1 1¾oz/50g skein (each approx 64yd/58m) of Lion Brand Yarn Fun Fur (polyester) each in #204 Lava (D) (5)

- Small amount of pale pink yarn for mouth
- One pair size 8 (5mm) needles, OR SIZE TO OBTAIN GAUGE
- 2 silver beads for eyes
- Stitch markers
- Polyester stuffing
- Tapestry needle

Gauge

16 sts and 22 rows to 4"/10cm over St st using size 8 (5mm) needles.
TAKE TIME TO CHECK GAUGE.

Note

When changing colors, twists yarns on WS to prevent holes in work. Use a separate length (or butterflies) of yarn for each block of color.

Square

(approx 11"/28cm square)
With A, cast on 16 sts; with C, cast on 6 sts; with B, cast on 1 st; with a 2nd length or butterfly of C, cast on 6 sts, with a 2nd length or butterfly of A, cast on 16 sts—45 sts in total.
Work in St st (k on RS, p on WS) and follow chart for 60 rows. Bind off.

Ears (make 2)

With A, cast on 7 sts
Rows 1–4 Knit.
Rows 5 and 7 Ssk, k to last 2 sts, k2tog—3 sts at end of row 7.
Row 6 Knit.
Row 8 SK2P. Secure last st.

Tail

With A and D held tog, cast on 15 sts.
Note Carry yarns not in use along side of work, twisting around working yarn every other row, to avoid cutting and weaving in ends.
Rows 1–4 With A & D, beg with a knit row, work in St st.
Rows 5–8 With C, work in St st.
Rows 9 and 10 With A & D, work in St st.
Row 11 (RS) With A & D, [k2, kfb in next st] 4 times, k3—19 sts.
Row 12 With A & D, purl.
Rows 13–16 With C, work in St st.
Rows 17 and 18 With A & D, work in St st.
Row 19 (RS) With A & D, [k2, kfb in next st] 6 times, k1—25 sts.
Row 20 With A & D, purl.
Rows 21–24 With C, work in St st.
Rows 25 & 27 With A & D, work in St st.
Row 27 (RS) With A & D, [k4, k2tog] 4 times, k1—19 sts.
Row 28 With A & D, purl.

Rows 29–32 With C, work in St st.
Rows 33 and 34 With A & D, work in St st.
Row 35 With A & D, [k1, k2tog] 6 times, k1—13 sts.
Row 36 With A & D, purl.
Rows 37–40 With C, work in St st.
Rows 41 and 42 With A & D, work in St st.
Row 43 With A & D, k1, [k2tog] 6 times—7 sts.
Row 44 With A & D, purl.
Rows 45 and 46 With C, work in St st.
Row 47 With C, k2, SK2P, k2—5 sts.
Row 48 With C, purl.
Row 49 K1, SK2P, k1—3 sts.
Row 50 With A & D, purl.
Row 51 SK2P. Secure last st.

....

Assembly

Lay square on a flat surface.
Mark the center 13 sts along cast-on edge.
Mark center st, measure up 20 rows from center st and place another marker. Cut a piece of yarn approx 25"/63.5cm long and sew running sts to outline the head, following the diagram for placement and leaving a long length at both ends.
Place markers along each side edge at 20 rows from cast-on and bound-off edges to mark one half of each leg.
Mark center 23 sts for butt.
Thread a length of yarn through these sts, leaving a long length as both ends.

Head

Pull both ends of the running-st yarn that marked the head, gathering the fabric until the outer edges meet at the center, then tie the ends in a double knot tightly. Stuff the head firmly. Fold head in half, pin and sew cast-on sts tog for chin seam.

Front Legs

Fold one front leg so that side edges (blue dotted lines) meet and form a point at the outer edge (toe), easing the longer side into the shorter side, and pin the edges tog. Sew the side edges together. Fold and sew the other front leg in same way. Stuff the legs firmly. Wrap a length of A about 3 times around tip of legs to create feet.

Back Legs

Work same as front legs following the green dotted lines.

Butt

Pull both ends of the yarn that marked the butt, gathering the fabric, then tie the ends in a double knot.
Be sure that the yarn is pulled tightly.

Tummy

Stuff the remainder of the body firmly. Pin the remaining two sides together and sew the tummy seam.

Finishing Details

With C, embroider three long straight stitches in center front of each ear.
Sew ears to head, approx 1"/2.5cm apart.
Sew tail seam and sew tail in place.
Sew on beads for eyes.
With B, embroider small straight sts for nose.
With pink, embroider straight sts for mouth. ✿

Dylan the Dachshund

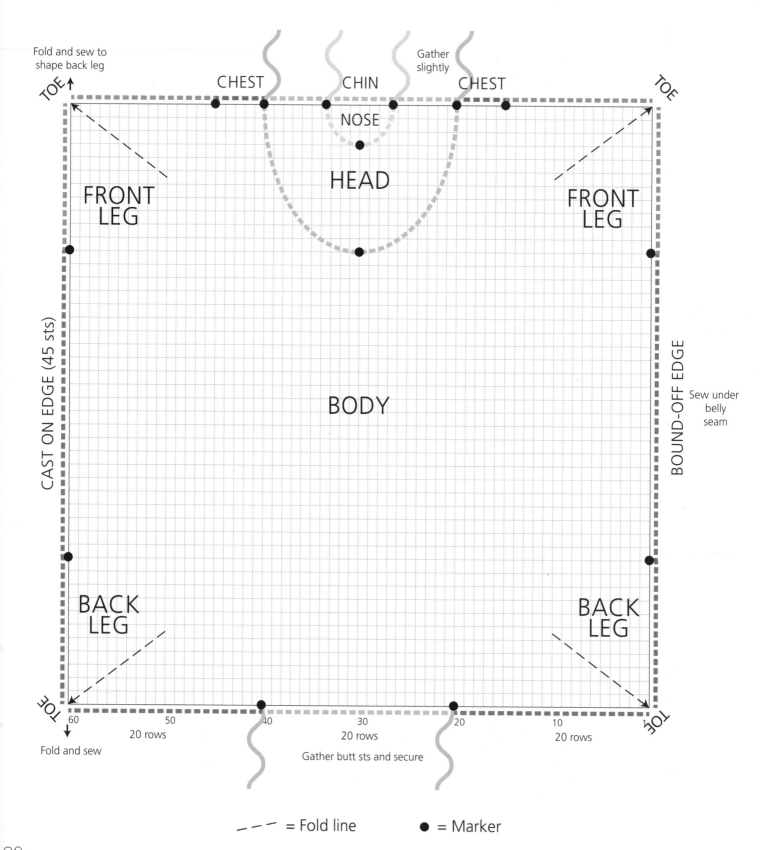

Fold and sew to
shape back leg

TOE↑

CHEST   CHIN   Gather
                          slightly
                    CHEST   TOE

NOSE

FRONT
LEG
                    HEAD   FRONT
                                              LEG

CAST ON EDGE (45 sts)

BODY

BOUND-OFF EDGE

Sew under
belly
seam

BACK
LEG
                                              BACK
                                              LEG

TOE

60   50   40   30   20   10   TOE↓

20 rows   20 rows   20 rows

Fold and sew

Gather butt sts and secure

- - - = Fold line   ● = Marker

90

Yippee ki-yay!
Git along little doggie!
Dachshunds are clever,
courageous, fun to knit,
and will be your best friend.

Materials
- 1 3½oz/100g ball (each approx 200yd/180m) of Plymouth Encore Worsted (acrylic/wool) in #1445 Brown (MC) 4
- Small amount in #0217 (CC)
- **One pair size 8 (5mm) needles, OR SIZE TO OBTAIN GAUGE**
- **Two size 7 (4.5mm) double-pointed needles (dpn) for tail only**
- **Two black beads for eyes**
- **Small length of red ribbon, ¼"/22cm wide**
- **Stitch markers**
- **Polyester stuffing**
- **Tapestry needle**

Gauge
18 sts and 24 rows to 4"/10cm over St st using size 8 (5mm) needles.
TAKE TIME TO CHECK GAUGE

Square
(approx 10"/25.5cm square)
With MC, cast on 45 sts. Work in St st (k on RS, p on WS) for 60 rows. Bind off.

Ears (make 2)
With MC, cast on 7 sts.
Row 1 (RS) K1, *p1, k1; rep from * to end.
Row 2 (WS) P1, *k1, p1; rep from * to end.
Rows 3–10 Rep rows 1 and 2 four times.
Row 11 (RS) K1, p1, SK2P, k1, p1—5 sts.
Rows 12 and 14 Rep row 2.
Row 13 Rep row 1.
Row 15 (RS) K1, SK2P, k1—3 sts.
Row 16 P3.
Row 17 SK2P. Secure last st.

Tail
With dpn and MC, cast on 3 sts.
*Row 1 (RS) Knit. Do *not* turn work. Slide the sts back to the opposite end of needle to work next row from RS. Pull yarn tightly from the end of the row. Rep from * for 18 rows. Change to CC, work 5 more rows. SK2P. Secure last stitch.

. . . .

Assembly
Note Shape dog's body by using big tapestry needle to distribute stuffing—bigger shoulders, smaller rear.
Mark the center 23 sts along and cast-on and bound-off edges (red dotted lines) for under belly. Mark the center 20 rows along one edge. Measure up 11 sts from the center of this edge and place a marker. Cut a piece of yarn approx 25"/63.5cm long and sew running sts to outline the head, following the diagram for placement and leaving a long length at both ends. Measure up 3 sts from center and place another marker for nose. Cut a piece of yarn approx 15"/38cm long and sew running sts to outline the nose, following the diagram for placement and leaving a long length at both ends. Mark the center 20 rows along the other edge for butt. Thread a length of yarn through these rows, leaving a long length as both ends.

Head
Pull both ends of the running-st yarn that marked the head, gathering the fabric until the outer edges meet at the center, then tie the ends in a double knot tightly. Stuff the head up to the nose firmly. Pull both ends of the running-st yarn that marked the nose, gathering the fabric slightly. Finish stuffing the nose.
Fold head in half, pin and sew cast-on sts tog for chin seam.

Butt
Pull both ends of the running-st yarn that marked the head, gathering the fabric until the outer edges meet at the center, then tie the ends in a double knot tightly.

Front Legs
Fold one front leg so that side edges (blue dotted lines) meet and form a point at the outer edge (toe), easing the longer side into the shorter side, and pin the edges together. Sew the side edges together. Fold and sew the other front leg in same way. Stuff the legs tightly.

Back Legs
Work same as front legs.

Belly
Stuff the remainder of the body firmly. Pin the remaining two sides together and sew the belly seam.

Finishing Details
Sew ears to head, leaving approx 1¼"/ 4.5cm between the ears (use photo as a guide). Sew tail to top of butt.
Sew on beads for eyes. With CC, embroider duplicate st over 1 st and 2 rows under the bead. With CC, embroider nose and mouth with straight sts.
Wrap and secure ribbon around neck. ✿

Oscar the Octopus

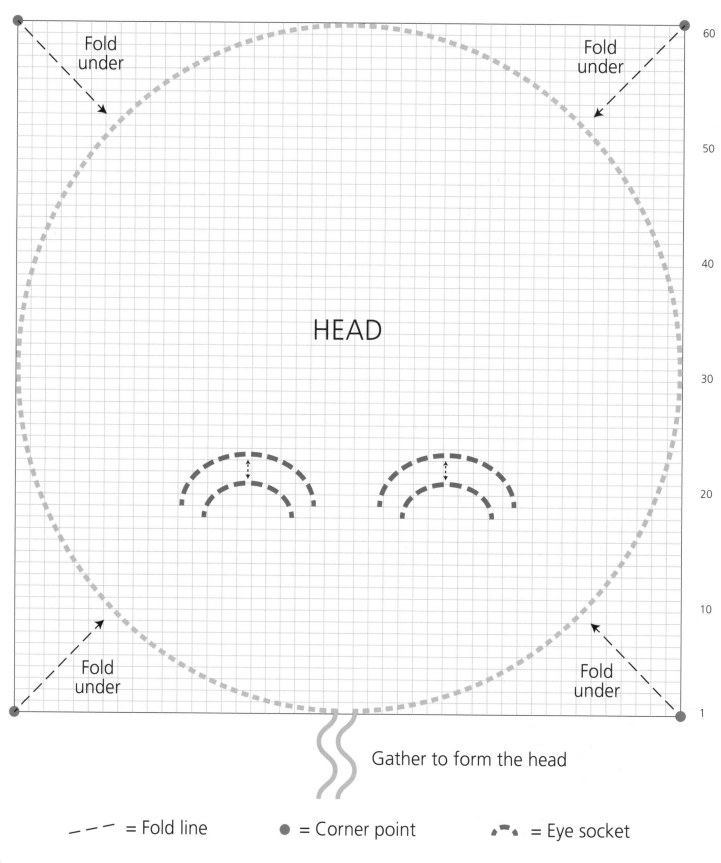

Fold under

Fold under

60

50

HEAD

40

30

20

10

Fold under

Fold under

1

Gather to form the head

– – – = Fold line   ● = Corner point   ⌒⌒ = Eye socket

94

Brave Oscar uses his eight tentacles to guard his sunken treasure at the bottom of the sea.

Materials
- 1 3½oz/100g balls (each approx 210yd/193m) of Madelinetosh Tosh Vintage (merino wool) in Penumbra (A) 【4】
- Small amount in Rose (B) for under-belly and eyes
- One pair size 8 (5mm) needles, OR SIZE TO OBTAIN GAUGE
- Two size 8 (5mm) double-pointed needles (dpn) for tentacles only
- Two purple beads and two smaller clear beads for eyes
- Stitch markers
- Polyester stuffing
- Tapestry needle

Gauge
18 sts and 24 rows to 4"/10cm over St st using size 8 (5mm) needles.
TAKE TIME TO CHECK GAUGE.

Stitch Glossary
MB (Make Bobble) [Knit into front and back of st] twice—4 sts made from 1 st; turn, p4 turn, k4, pass 2nd, 3rd, 4th sts, one at a time over first st.

Square
(approx 10"/25.5cm square)
With A, cast on 45 sts. Work in St st (k on RS, p on WS) for 60 rows. Bind off.

Tentacles
*With A and dpn, cast on 5 sts. Work bobble I-cord as foll:
Row 1 (RS) K5, without turning work, slide the sts back to the opposite end of needle to work next row from RS. Pull yarn tightly from the end of the row.
Rows 2–5 Rep row 1.
Row 6 K2, MB, k2, do *not* turn, slide sts to opposite end of needle.
Rep rows 1–6 three more times, then work rows 1–5 once more.

Place sts on spare needle.
Rep from * for bobble I-cord 7 more times.
Do *not* cut yarn on last tentacle (8 tentacles on the spare needle).
With RS facing, k across all 40 sts. Purl 1 row, knit 1 row, purl 1 row. Bind off.

Bobble for Eyes (make 2)
With B, make a slipknot, knit into front, back, front, back and front of st—5 sts.
Rows 1 and 3 (WS) Purl.
Row 2 Knit.
Row 4 (RS) SKP, k1, k2tog—3 sts.
Row 5 Purl.
Row 6 SK2P. Secure last st.

Under Belly
With B, cast on 32 sts over 2 needles for a loose cast-on. Remove one needle.
Knit 4 rows.
Next row [K2tog] 16 times—16 sts.
Pass all sts over the first st and off the needle one at a time.

Assembly
Lay square on a flat surface.
Baste around square following yellow dotted line on diagram, leaving a long length at both ends.
Gather to form the head.
Stuff and secure the gather at the neck, leaving approx 2"/5cm opening.
Fold and stitch four corner points (red dots on diagram) under the gather and secure.

Finishing Details
Following diagram, for each eye socket, pinch the fabric to create a half moon shape and stitch through both thicknesses to secure (purple dotted lines).
Sew beads to the center of bobbles.
Sew bobbles to the eye sockets.
Sew tentacles around neck at the gather.
Insert under belly into opening of neck and sew in place. ✿

Zoe the Zebra

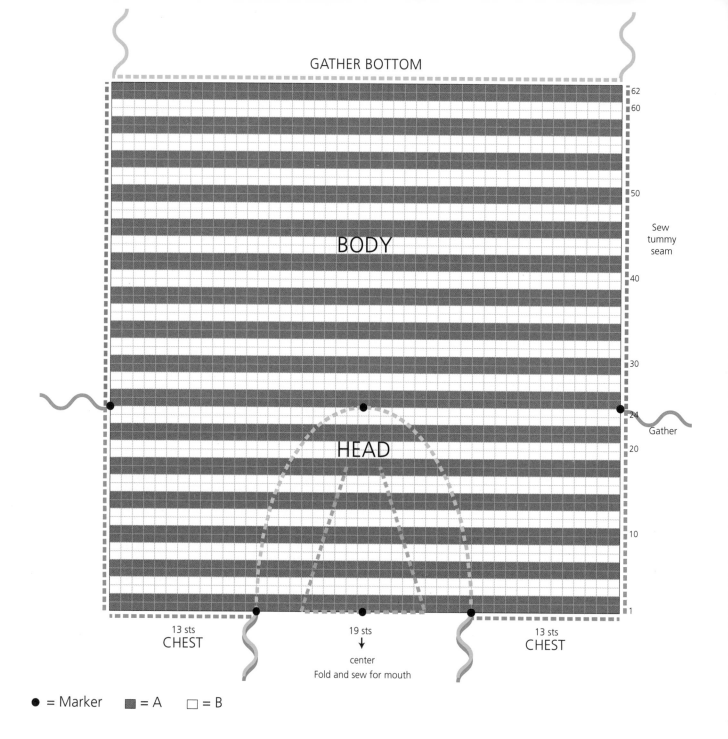

GATHER BOTTOM

BODY

HEAD

62
60

50

40

30

24
20

10

1

Sew tummy seam

Gather

13 sts
CHEST

19 sts
↓
center
Fold and sew for mouth

13 sts
CHEST

● = Marker   ■ = A   □ = B

Black and white stripes are so hot right now. Every zebra, including Zoe, is wearing them!

Materials
- 1 3½oz/100g ball (each approx 220yd/200m) of Cascade 220 Superwash (superwash wool) each in #815 Black (A) and #871 White (B) (4)
- One pair size 7 (4.5mm) needles, OR SIZE TO OBTAIN GAUGE
- Two size 7 (4.5mm) double-pointed needles (dpn)
- Two black beads for eyes
- Stitch markers
- Polyester stuffing
- Tapestry needle

Gauges

18 sts and 24 rows to 4"/10cm over St st using size 7 (4.5mm) needles.
TAKE TIME TO CHECK GAUGE.

Stripe Pattern

Row 1 (RS) With A, knit.
Row 2 With A, purl.
Row 3 With B, knit.
Row 4 With B, purl.
Rep rows 1–4 for stripe pat.

Square

(approx 10"/25.5cm square)
With A, cast on 45 sts. Work in stripe pat for 62 rows, ending with 2 rows A.
Bind off with A.

Legs

With B, cast on 8 sts for hoof. Work 8 rows in St st. Change to A and work in stripe pat for 22 rows (11 stripes). Bind off.
Sew seam and stuff as you sew.
Gather cast-on edge of hoof and secure.

Ears

With A, cast on 5 sts.
Beg with a k row, work in St st for 4 rows.
Row 5 (RS) K1, SK2P, k1—3 sts.
Row 6 Purl.
Row 7 SK2P. Secure last st.

Stitch Glossary

LS (Loop Stitch) Worked on wrong side.
Insert RH needle into st as if to knit it.
Wind yarn over RH needle and around index finger of left hand 3 times, then over RH needle point once more. Draw all loops through st on LH needle, then slip loops to LH needle. Insert RH needle through back of these loops and original st and knit them together through back loops.

Mane

With 1 strand each A and B held tog, cast on 17 sts.
Next row (WS) *K1, LS; rep from * to last st, k1. Bind off.

Tail

With dpn and A, cast on 3 sts.
***Row 1 (RS)** Knit. Do *not* turn work.
Slide the sts back to the opposite end of needle to work next row from RS. Pull yarn tightly from the end of the row.
Rep from *, working in stripe pat, for 16 rows (8 stripes).
Next row (RS) With A, knit. Turn work.
Next row With A, SK2P. Secure last st.
For tip of tail, with 1 strand each A & B held tog, cast on 3 sts. K1, work loop st in next st same as on mane, k1. Bind off.
Sew loop to bound-off edge of tail.

. . . .

Assembly

Lay square on a flat surface.
Mark the center 19 sts as along cast-on edge. Place marker on center st on cast-on edge, then measure up 24 rows from center marker and place another marker.
Cut a piece of yarn approx 25"/63.5cm long and sew running sts to outline the head, following the diagram for placement (yellow dotted lines) and leaving a long length at both ends. Thread tapestry needle and sew running stitches along bound-off sts for bottom, leaving long tails at each end.
Count up 24 rows from cast-on edge at each side and place markers. Thread tapestry needle and sew running stitches along 24 rows and 13 cast-on sts each side for chest (blue dotted lines).

Bottom and Tummy

Pull both ends of the running-st yarn that marked the bottom. Gather the sts tightly and secure. Sew tummy seam along red dotted lines. Secure. Stuff body.

Head

Pull both ends of the running-st yarn that marked the head, pull together, stuff and shape the head.
Stitch the head from side to side for 9 stripes to shape (green dotted lines).
Secure yarn. Sew nose/mouth closed.

Chest

Pull both ends of the running-st yarn that marked the chest and gather, sew chest fronts together to close.

Finishing Details

Sew on legs (see photo).
Sew mane to center top of head.
Sew on ears either side of mane and sew tail to center of back.
Sew on beads for eyes. ❀

Amadeus the Fox

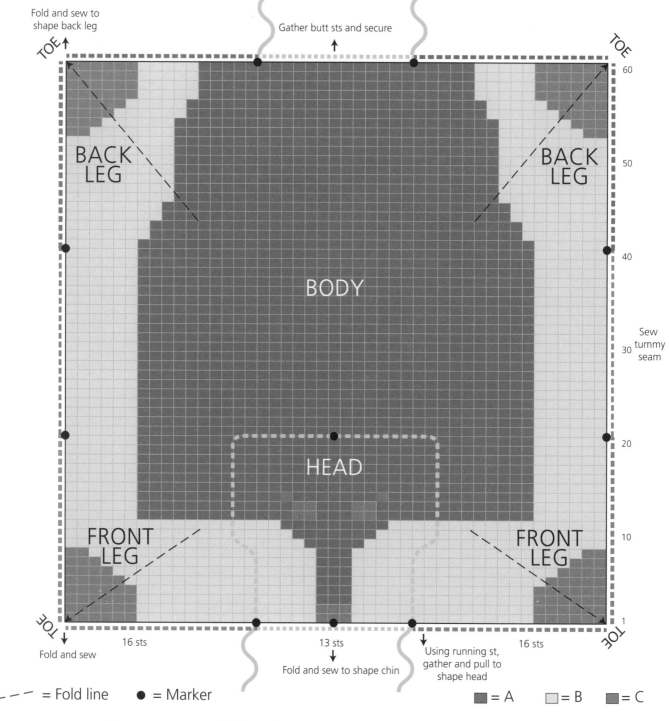

Fold and sew to shape back leg

Gather butt sts and secure

TOE

TOE

BACK LEG

BACK LEG

60

50

BODY

Sew tummy seam

40

30

HEAD

20

FRONT LEG

FRONT LEG

10

TOE

TOE

Fold and sew

16 sts

13 sts

Fold and sew to shape chin

Using running st, gather and pull to shape head

16 sts

1

_ _ _ = Fold line   ● = Marker

■ = A   □ = B   ■ = C

Never try to outfox a fox, but you don't need to be sly to bring Amadeus to life.

Materials
- 1 3½oz/100g skein (each approx 200yd/180m) of Plymouth Yarn Encore (acrylic/wool) each #1445 Burnished Heather (Rust–A), #0240 Taupe (B) and #0217 Black (C) 〔4〕
- One pair size 8 (5mm) needles, OR SIZE TO OBTAIN GAUGE
- Size H/8 (5mm) crochet hook for attaching whiskers
- 2 black beads for eyes
- Stitch markers
- Polyester stuffing
- Tapestry needle

Gauge
18 sts and 24 rows to 4"/10cm over St st using size 8 (5mm) needles.
TAKE TIME TO CHECK GAUGE.

Note
When working chart, use separate lengths (butterflies) of yarn for each block of color and when changing colors, twist yarns on WS to prevent holes in work.

Stitch Glossary
LS (Loop Stitch) Worked on wrong side. Insert RH needle into st as if to knit it. Wind yarn over RH needle and around index finger of left hand 3 times, then over RH needle point once more. Draw all loops through st on LH needle, then slip loops to LH needle.Insert RH needle through back of these loops and original st and knit them together through back loops.

Square
(approx 10"/25.5cm square)
With C, cast on 6 sts; with B, cast on 15 sts; with a 2nd length or butterfly of C, cast on 3 sts; with a 2nd length or butterfly of B, cast on 15 sts, with 3rd length or butterfly of C, cast on 6 sts—45 sts in total. Work in St st (k on RS, p on WS) and follow chart for 60 rows. Bind off.

Ears (make 2)
With A, cast on 9 sts.
Work in St st for 4 rows.
Row 5 (RS) K2, ssk, k1, k2tog, k2—7 sts.
Row 6 Purl.
Row 7 K1, ssk, k1, k2tog, k1—5 sts.
Row 8 Purl.
Row 9 Ssk, k1, k2tog—3 sts.
Row 10 Purl.
Row 11 SK2P. Secure last st.

Tail
With A, cast on 15 sts. Work in rev St st (p on RS, k on WS) for 7 rows.
Row 8 (WS) K1, [LS, k1] 7 times.
Row 9 Purl.
Row 10 K2, [LS, k1] 6 times, k1.

Row 11 Purl.
Rows 12–26 Rep rows 8–11 three times, then rows 8–10 once more.
Row 27 P1, p2tog, p to last 3 sts, p2tog, p1—13 sts.
Rows 28–38 Rep rows 8–11 twice, then rows 8–10 once more.
Row 39 [P1, p2tog] 4 times, p1—9 sts.
Rows 30–33 Rep rows 8–11 once.
Cut A, change to B.
Rows 34–36 Rep rows 8–10.
Row 37 [P2tog] 4 times, p1—5 sts.
Row 38 Rep row 8.
Row 39 [P2tog] twice, p1—3 sts.
Row 40 K1, LS, k1.
Row 41 Slip1, p2tog, psso. Secure last st.

. . . .

Assembly
Lay square on a flat surface.
Mark the center 13 sts along cast-on edge. Mark center st, measure up 20 rows from center st and place another marker. Cut a piece of yarn approx 25"/63.5cm long and sew running sts to outline head, following the diagram for placement and leaving a long length at both ends. Place markers along each side edge at 20 rows from cast-on and bound-off edges to mark one half of leg. Mark center 13 sts along bound-off edge.

Head
Pull both ends of the running-st yarn that marked the head, gathering the fabric until the outer edges meet at the center, then tie the ends in a double knot tightly. Stuff the head firmly. Fold head in half, pin and sew cast-on sts tog for chin seam.

Front Legs
Fold one front leg so that side edges (blue dotted lines) meet and form a point at the outer edge (toe), easing the longer side into the shorter side, and pin the edges together. Sew the side edges together. Fold and sew the other front leg in same way. Stuff the legs firmly.

Butt
Pull both ends of the yarn that marked

the butt, gathering the fabric, then tie the ends in a double knot.
Be sure that the yarn is pulled tightly.

Back Legs
Fold one back leg so that side edges meet (green dotted lines) and form a point at the outer edge and pin the edges together. Sew the side edges together. Fold and sew the other back leg in same way. Stuff the legs firmly.

Tummy
Stuff the remainder of the body firmly. Pin the remaining two sides together and sew the tummy seam.

Finishing Details
With C, embroider three long straight stitches in center front each ear. Sew ears to head, approx 1"/2.5cm apart. Sew tail seam and stuff lightly. Sew tail in place. Sew on beads for eyes.
To make whiskers, cut twelve 4"/10cm long strips of A.
With crochet hook fold two strips in half and attach to fox's face making one fringe. Make three on each side (see photo). ✾

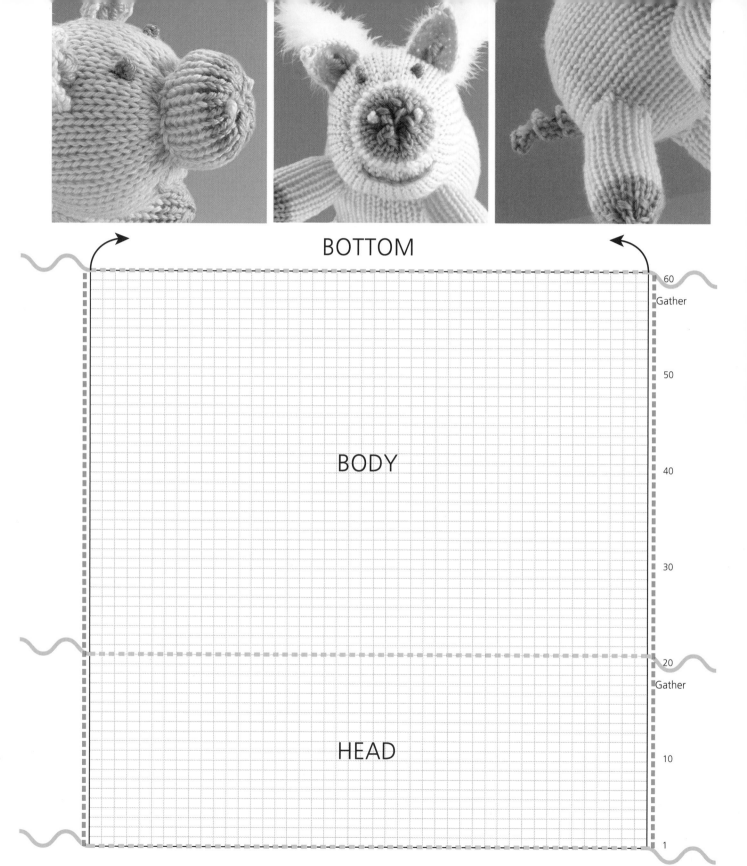

BOTTOM

BODY

HEAD

60
Gather

50

40

30

20
Gather

10

1

Gather

Pretty in pink, Paloma flies through the clouds. Her aerobatics prove pigs really can fly!

Materials
- 1 3½oz/100g ball (each approx 213yd/195m) of Cascade Pacific (acrylic/superwash wool) each in #18 Cotton Candy (Light Pink–A) and #52 Geranium (Dark Pink–B) (4)
- Small amount of blue yarn for eyes
- One pair size 7 (4.5mm) needles, OR SIZE TO OBTAIN GAUGE
- Small length of purple ribbon 1½"/4cm wide
- 5"/12.5cm angel wings (found at craft stores)
- Stitch markers
- Polyester stuffing
- Tapestry needle

Gauge
18 sts and 24 rows to 4"/10cm over St st using size 7 (4.5mm) needles.
TAKE TIME TO CHECK GAUGE.

Square
(approx 10"/25.5cm square)
With A, cast on 45 sts. Work in St st (k on RS, p on WS) for 60 rows. Bind off.

Ears (make 2)
With A, cast on 9 sts.
Rows 1–4 Beg with a RS row, work in St st.
Row 5 (RS) K3, SK2P, k3—7 sts.
Row 6 Purl.
Row 7 K2, SK2P, k2—5 sts.
Row 8 Purl.
Row 9 K1, SK2P, k1—3 sts.
Row 10 Slip 1, p2tog, psso. Secure last st.

Legs (make 4)
With A, cast on 15 sts. Work in St st for 14 rows. Cut A, change to B and work 4 rows.
Next row (RS) [K2tog] 7 times, k1—8 sts.
Next row [P2tog] 4 times—4 sts.
Slip all sts over the first one at a time and off the needle. Secure last st.
Sew seam and stuff legs.

Snout
With A, cast on 20 sts. Work in St st for 6 rows. Cut A, change to B and work 4 rows.
Next row (RS) [K2tog] 10 times—10 sts.
Next row (WS) [P2tog] 5 times—5 sts.
Pass 2nd, 3rd, 4th and 5th sts over first st and off the needle. Secure last st.

Tail
With B, cast on 20 sts. K into front, back, and front of every st. Bind off purlwise. Twist tightly to shape into a coil.

Assembly
Thread tapestry needle and sew running stitches along cast-on and bound-off edges for bottom, leaving long tails at each end. Count up 20 rows from cast-on edge and work running sts along this row, leaving long tails at each end (see orange dotted lines on schematic).
Fold piece in half so that side edges meet (two blue lines) and sew tummy seam. Gather bound-off sts for bottom, then stuff body. Gather the thread at 20 rows above the cast-on edge for neck, then stuff the head. Gather cast on edge to close the head. Stuff the nose and sew to front of face (see photo). With A, embroider French knots to snout for nostrils. Sew on ears, approx 1"/2.5cm apart. With blue yarn, embroider French knots for eyes. Stuff and sew legs to body (see photo). Sew tail to center of bottom.
Tie purple ribbon around neck. Secure wings to back just below the neck. ❁

Armando the Armadillo

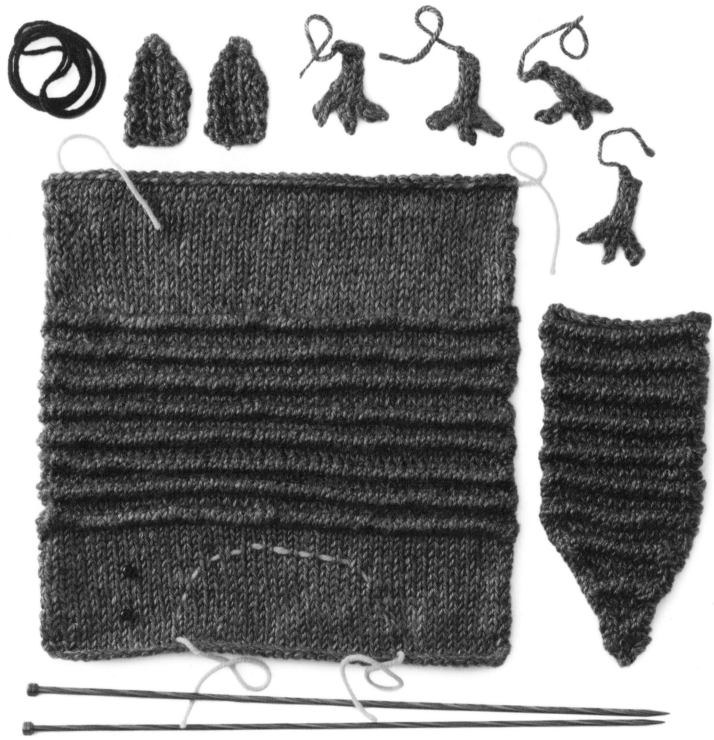

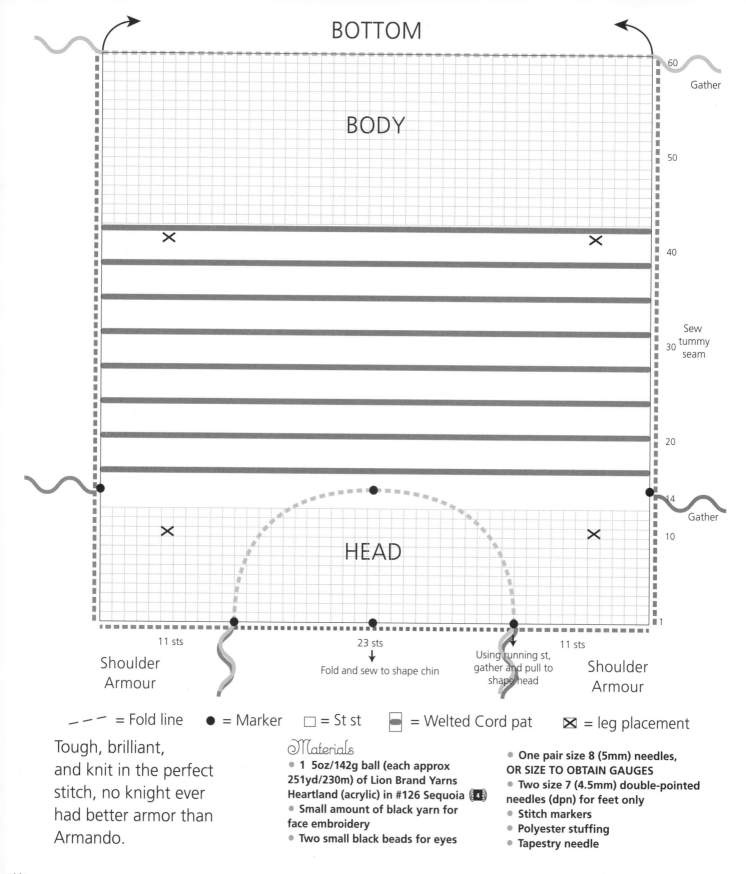

BOTTOM

BODY

60

Gather

50

40

Sew
tummy
seam

30

20

14

Gather

10

HEAD

1

11 sts

23 sts
↓
Fold and sew to shape chin

Using running st,
gather and pull to
shape head

11 sts

Shoulder
Armour

Shoulder
Armour

- - - = Fold line   ● = Marker   □ = St st   ▬ = Welted Cord pat   ⊠ = leg placement

Tough, brilliant,
and knit in the perfect
stitch, no knight ever
had better armor than
Armando.

Materials
- 1 5oz/142g ball (each approx 251yd/230m) of Lion Brand Yarns Heartland (acrylic) in #126 Sequoia (4)
- Small amount of black yarn for face embroidery
- Two small black beads for eyes
- One pair size 8 (5mm) needles, OR SIZE TO OBTAIN GAUGES
- Two size 7 (4.5mm) double-pointed needles (dpn) for feet only
- Stitch markers
- Polyester stuffing
- Tapestry needle

Gauges

- 18 sts and 24 rows to 4"/10cm over St st using size 8 (5mm) needles.
- 18 sts and 48 rows to 4"/10cm over welted cord pat using size 8 (5mm) needles.

TAKE TIME TO CHECK GAUGES.

Welted Cord Pattern

Rows 1, 3, 5 and 7 (RS) Knit.

Rows 2, 4 and 6 K1, p to last st, k1.

Row 8 (cording row) K1, *with yarn in front, insert needle from the top down into the head of the purl st 4 rows below the next st on needle; pick up this loop, place it on LH needle and purl it together with next st; rep from * on every st across row to last st, end k1.

Repeat rows 1–8 for welted cord pat.

Square

(approx 10"/25.5cm square)

Cast on 45 sts.

Beg with a k row, work 12 rows in St st (k on RS, p on WS).

Rep rows 1–8 of welted cord pat 8 times.

Beg with a k row, work 18 rows in St st, or until piece measure 10"/25.5cm. Bind off.

Tail

Cast on 15 sts. Rep rows 1–8 of welted cord pat 7 times. Cont in pat as foll:

Rows 1 and 2 Work even in pat.

Row 3 Ssk, k to last 2 sts, k2tog—2 sts dec'd.

Rows 4–6 Work even in pat.

Row 7 Rep row 3.

Row 8 Work cording row.

Rep last 8 rows until 3 sts rem, end with a WS row.

Last row SK2P. Secure last st.

Sew seam and stuff lightly.

Ears (make 2)

Cast on 9 sts.

Rows 1, 3 and 5 (RS) *K1, p1; rep from *, end k1.

Rows 2, 4 and 6 (WS) P1, *k1, p1; rep from * to end.

Cont in k1, p1 rib as foll:

Row 7 (RS) Ssk, work to last 2 sts, k2tog—7 sts.

Row 8 Work even in rib.

Rep last 2 rows 2 more times—3 sts.

Row 13 SK2P. Secure last st.

Feet (make 4)

Make a slipknot and place on dpn.

Rows 1–3 Cast on 4 sts, bind off 4 sts, slip st to LH needle—3 toes made at end of row 3.

Row 4 (RS) Pick up 3 sts along base of toes—4 sts. Do *not* turn.

Work I-cord as foll:

*Row 1 (RS) Knit. Do *not* turn work.

Slide the sts back to the opposite end of needle to work next row from RS.

Pull yarn tightly from the end of the row.

Rep from * for 1"/2.5cm.

Bind off. Secure last st.

. . . .

Assembly

Lay square on a flat surface.

Mark the center 23 sts as along cast-on edge. Mark center st and measure up 14 rows from center st and place another marker. Cut a piece of yarn approx 25"/63.5cm long and sew running sts to outline the head, foll the diagram for placement and leaving a long length at both ends. Thread tapestry needle and sew running stitches along bound-off sts for bottom, leaving long tails at each end.

Count up 14 rows from cast-on edge at each side. Thread tapestry needle and sew running stitches along 14 rows and 11 cast-on sts each side for shoulder armor (blue dotted lines).

Head

Pull both ends of the running-st yarn that marked the head, gathering the fabric until the outer edges meet at the center, then tie the ends in a double knot tightly. Stuff the head firmly. Fold head in half, pin and sew cast-on sts tog for chin seam.

Bottom and Tummy

Pull both ends of the running-st yarn that marked the bottom. Gather the sts tightly and secure. Sew tummy seam along red dotted lines. Secure. Stuff body.

Shoulder Armor

Pull both ends of the running-st yarn that marked the shoulder armor.

Gather and stuff to shape armor on each side and secure.

Sew each gather together at center front.

Finishing Details

Sew tail to center of bottom.

Sew cast-on edge of ears to back neck, with the lower edges meeting at the center.

Sew feet to body, see x's on diagram for placement.

Sew beads for eyes and with black yarn, embroider brows and mouth. ❀

Liam the Lion

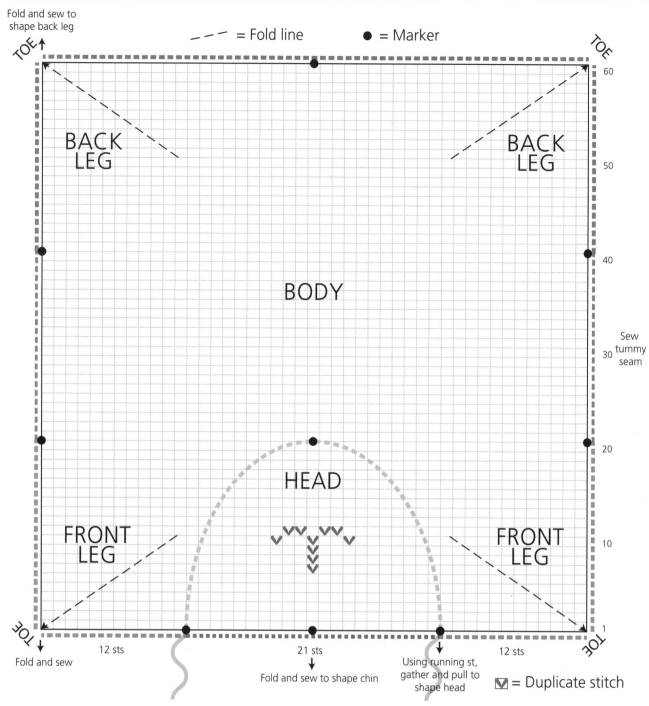

Fold and sew to shape back leg

= Fold line   ● = Marker

TOE

BACK LEG

BACK LEG

TOE

60

50

40

BODY

Sew tummy seam

30

20

HEAD

10

FRONT LEG

FRONT LEG

TOE

TOE

1

12 sts

Fold and sew

21 sts

Fold and sew to shape chin

Using running st, gather and pull to shape head

12 sts

☑ = Duplicate stitch

With his crown of gold, Liam can easily be king of your jungle and guard your yarn stash.

Materials
- 1 5oz/142g ball (each approx 251yd/230m) of Lion Brand Yarns Heartland (acrylic) each in #169 Shenandoah (A) and #124 Big Bend (B) (4)
- 1 .88oz/25g ball (each approx 109yd/100m) of Rowan Anchor Artiste Metallic (viscose/metallized polyester) in #300 Gold (C) (1)
- One pair size 8 (5mm) needles, OR SIZE TO OBTAIN GAUGE
- Two size 8 (5mm) double-pointed needles (dpn) for tail only
- Two size 3 (3.25mm) double-pointed needles (dpn) for crown only
- Small amount of black yarn and beige embroidery floss for face embroidery
- 2 beads for eyes
- Stitch markers
- Polyester stuffing
- Tapestry needle

Gauge

18 sts and 24 rows to 4"/10cm over St st using size 9 (5.5mm) needles.
TAKE TIME TO CHECK GAUGE.

Stitch Glossary

Loop Stitch (LS) Worked on wrong side. Insert RH needle into st as if to knit it. Wind yarn over RH needle and around index finger of left hand 3 times, then over RH needle point once more. Draw all loops through st on LH needle, then slip loops to LH needle. Insert RH needle through back of these loops and original st and knit them together through back loops.

Square

(approx 10"/28cm square)
With A, cast on 45 sts.
Work in St st (k on RS, p on WS) and for 60 rows. Bind off.
With B, embroider duplicate st following diagram.

Ears (make 2)

With A, cast on 7 sts.
Rows 1–4 Knit.
Row 5 Ssk, k to last 2 sts, k2tog—5 sts.
Row 6 Knit.
Row 7 Rep row 5—3 sts.
Row 8 SK2P.
Secure last st, leaving an end for attaching.

Manes

Outer mane With B, cast on 33 sts.
Next row (WS) K1, work LS in each st to last st, k1.
Bind off.
Longer inner mane With B, cast on 40 sts and work as for outer mane.
Front mane With B, cast on 25 sts and work as for outer mane.
Short front mane With B, cast on 10 sts and work as for outer mane.

Tail

With larger dpn and A, cast on 4 sts.
*Row 1 (RS) Knit. Do *not* turn work. Slide the sts back to the opposite end of needle to work next row from RS. Pull yarn tightly from the end of the row. Rep from * for

approx 6½"/16.5cm.
Bind off, leaving an end for attaching.
For tip of tail, with B, cast on 6 sts and work loop st as for outer mane.
Sew to bound-off edge of tail.

Crown (optional)

With smaller dpn and C, cast on 8 sts.
Row 1 Knit.
Row 2 Sl 1, k2, yo, k2tog, k1, [yo] 4 times, k2.
Row 3 Sl 1, k1, [k1, p1] twice into the 4 yo's, k3, yo, k2tog, k1.
Row 4 Sl 1, k2, yo, k2tog, k7.
Row 5 Sl 1, k8, yo, k2tog, k1.
Row 6 Sl 1, k2, yo, k2tog, k7.
Row 7 Bind off 4 sts, k4, yo, k2tog, k2.
Rep rows 2–7 nine more times—10 points in total. Bind off.
Sew cast-on and bound-off edges tog.

· ·

Assembly

Lay square on a flat surface.
Mark the center 21 sts along cast-on edge. Mark the center st and measure up 20 rows from center st and place another marker. Cut a piece of yarn approx 25"/63.5cm long and sew running sts to outline the head, following the diagram for placement and leaving a long length at both ends.
Place markers along each side edge at 20 rows from cast-on and bound-off edges to mark one half of each leg. Mark the center st along bound-off edge to mark other half of each back leg.

Head

Pull both ends of the running-st yarn that marked the head, gathering the fabric until the outer edges meet at the center, then tie the ends in a double knot tightly. Stuff the head firmly.
Fold head in half, pin and sew cast-on sts tog for chin seam.

Front Legs

Fold one front leg so that side edges (blue dotted lines) meet and form a point at the outer edge (toe), easing the longer side into the shorter side, and pin the edges together. Sew the side edges together.

Fold and sew the other front leg in same way. Stuff the legs firmly.

Back Legs

Fold one back leg so that side edges (green dotted lines) meet at the center marked st and form a point at the outer edge (toe) easing the longer side into the shorter side, and pin the edges together.
Sew the side edges together.
Fold and sew the other back leg in same way. Stuff the legs firmly.

Tummy

Stuff the remainder of the body firmly. Pin the remaining two sides together and sew the tummy seam.

Finishing Details

Sew short front mane to center at top of head. Sew front mane around neck closest to the head, then sew longer inner mane behind the front mane, then outer behind the inner mane.
Sew ears on either side of mane.
Sew tail to top of butt.
Sew on beads for eyes. With black yarn, embroider nose with satin st in center of face. Embroider mouth with straight sts. For whiskers, attach strands of embroidery floss on either side of the nose. ❁

Paco, Polly & Percival the Penguins

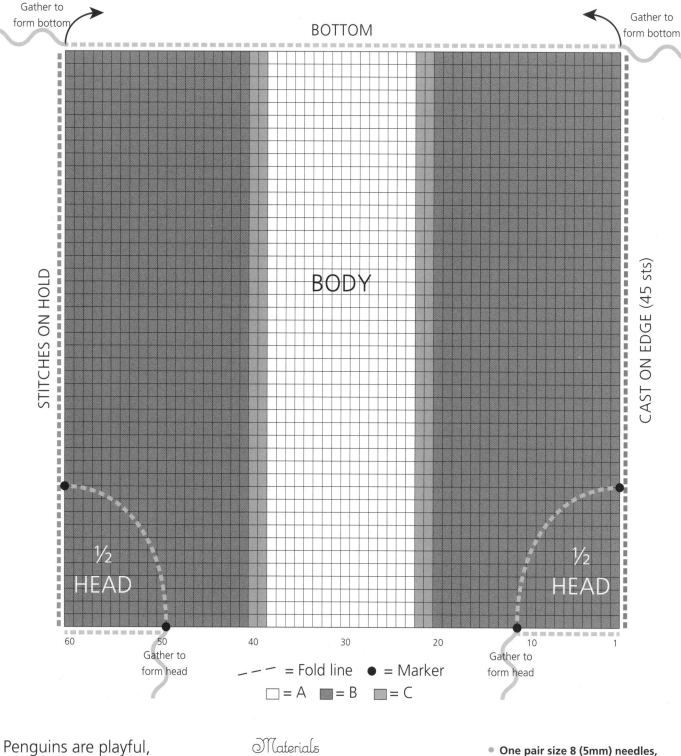

Gather to form bottom

BOTTOM

Gather to form bottom

STITCHES ON HOLD

CAST ON EDGE (45 sts)

BODY

½ HEAD

½ HEAD

60   50   40   30   20   10   1

Gather to form head

Gather to form head

– – – = Fold line   ● = Marker

☐ = A   ▦ = B   ▨ = C

Penguins are playful, but they always look so formal. Wouldn't it be fun to see them in sweaters?

Materials
- 1 3½oz/100g ball (each approx 220yd/200m) of Cascade 220 Superwash (superwash wool) each in #871 White (A), #815 Black (B) and #877 Golden (C) **④**

- One pair size 8 (5mm) needles, **OR SIZE TO OBTAIN GAUGE**
- 2 small black beads for eyes
- Stitch markers
- Polyester stuffing
- Tapestry needle

Gauge

18 sts and 24 rows to 4"/10cm over St st using size 8 (5mm) needles.
TAKE TIME TO CHECK GAUGE.

Provisional Cast-On

Note If you prefer not to use a provisional cast on, you can use a traditional cast-on. The provisional cast on was used here. Using scrap yarn and crochet hook, chain the number of sts to cast on plus a few extra. Cut a tail and pull the tail through the last chain. With knitting needle and yarn, pick up and knit the stated number of sts through the "purl bumps" on the back of the chain. To remove scrap yarn chain, when instructed, pull out the tail from the last crochet stitch.
Gently and slowly pull on the tail to unravel the crochet stitches, carefully placing each released knit stitch on a needle.

Square

(approx 10"/25.5cm square)
With B, cast on 45 sts using provisional cast on.
Rows 1–20 Work in St st (k on RS, p on WS). Cut B, join C.
Rows 21 and 22 With C, work in St st. Cut C, join A.
Rows 23–38 With A, work in St st. Cut A, join C.
Rows 39 and 40 With C, work in St st. Cut C, join B.
Rows 41–60 With B, work in St st. Do *not* bind off, leave sts on needle. (If using traditional cast on, bind off the sts).

Wings (make 2)

With B, cast on 5 sts.
Row 1 (RS) Kfb into each st—10 sts.
Row 2 Purl.
Rows 3–6 Work in St st.
Rows 7–12 (RS) *K1, p1; rep from * to end.
Row 13 Rib 4 sts, k2tog, rib 4 sts—9 sts.
Row 14 Rib 3 sts, SK2P, rib 3 sts—7 sts.
Row 15 Knit.
Row 16 Purl.
Row 17 K2, SK2P, k2—5 sts.
Row 18 Purl.
Row 19 K1, SK2P, k1—3 sts.
Row 20 Purl.
Row 21 SK2P. Secure last st.

Tail

With B, cast on 10 sts.
Work in k1, p1 rib for 1"/2.5cm.
Work rows 13–21 same as wings.

Feet-Talons

With B, make a slipknot and place on needle.
Rows 1–3 Cast on 4 sts, bind off 4 sts, slip st to LH needle—3 talons made at end of row 3.
Row 4 (RS) Pick up 3 sts along base of talons—4 sts.
Rows 5 and 7 Purl.
Row 6 Knit.
Row 8 [K2tog] twice—2 sts.
Row 9 P2tog. Secure last st.

. . . .

Assembly

Using Kitchener Stitch, join cast-on edge to sts on needle (if using a regular cast on, sew edges tog).
With tapestry needle and long length of B, loop all sts on one edge, pull tightly and secure for bottom of penguin (see orange dotted line on schematic).
Stuff ¾ of the way.
Mark center 22 black rows and count 11 sts down from center to mark top of head. Cut a piece of yarn approx 25"/63.5cm long and sew running sts to outline the head, following the diagram for placement and leaving a long length at both ends. Stuff the head firmly. Fold head in half, pin and sew cast-on sts tog for chin seam.

Finishing Details

Sew feet to bottom along the gold stripe.
Sew tail to center of back, approx 2"/5cm from the gathered bottom.
Sew wings to sides of body, a few rows outside the gold stripes (see photo).
Gather approx ¼"/2cm at tip of head and wrap C several times around to form beak.
With C, embroider mouth below beak.
Sew on beads for eyes.
With A, embroider straight st along sides of eyes. Tuck and stitch neck to chest, or leave head pointing upward. ✿

Abigail the Teddy Bear

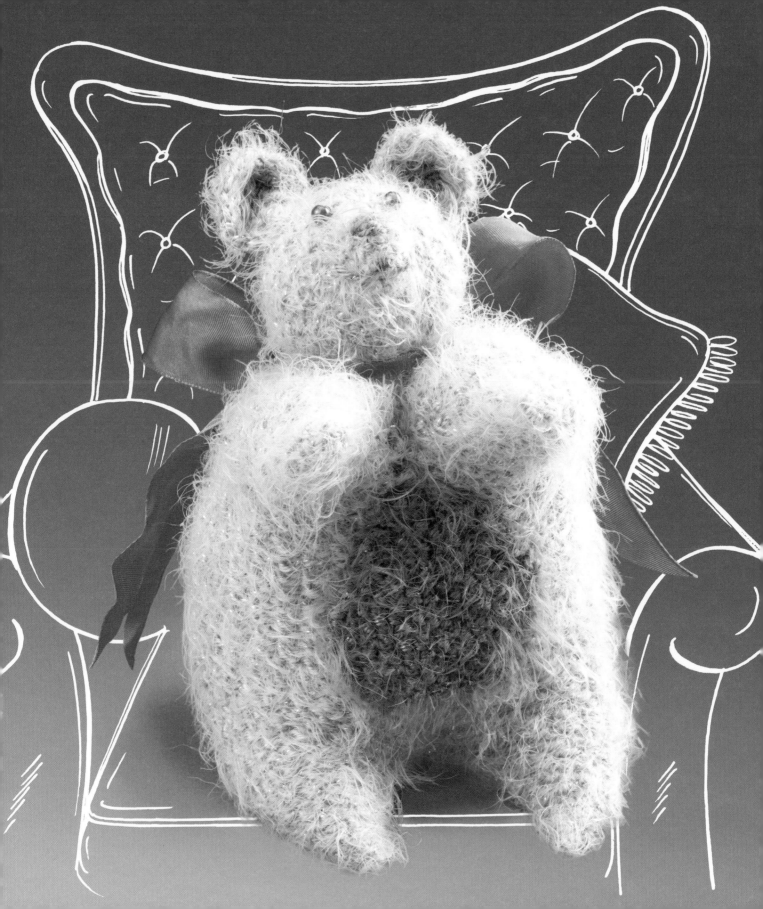

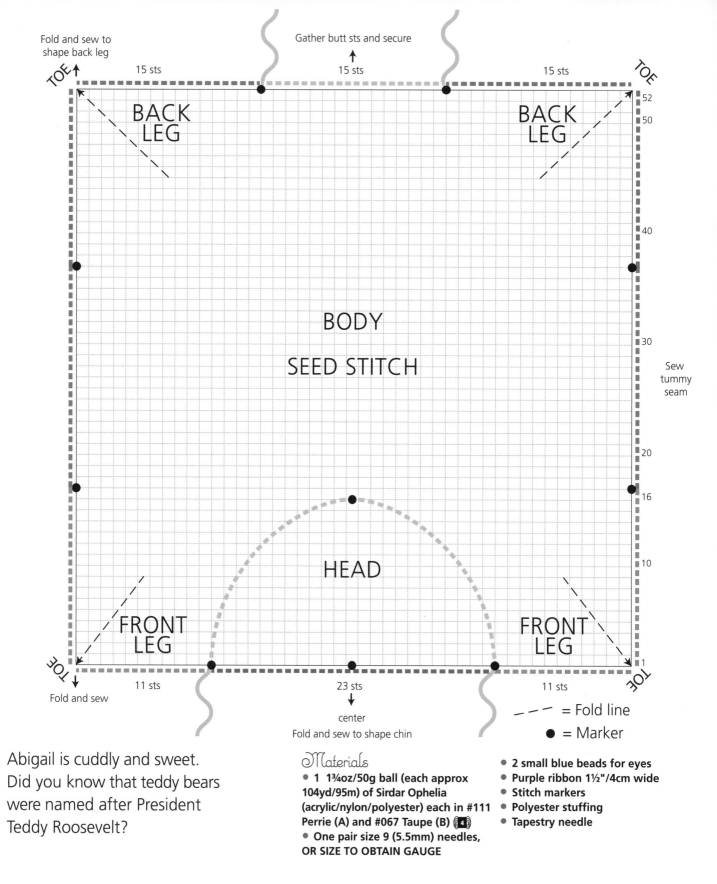

Fold and sew to shape back leg

Gather butt sts and secure

TOE ↑

BACK LEG

BACK LEG

TOE

15 sts   15 sts   15 sts

52
50

BODY

SEED STITCH

40

Sew tummy seam

30

HEAD

20

16

10

FRONT LEG

FRONT LEG

1

TOE

TOE

11 sts   23 sts   11 sts

Fold and sew

center
↓
Fold and sew to shape chin

‒ ‒ ‒ = Fold line
● = Marker

Abigail is cuddly and sweet. Did you know that teddy bears were named after President Teddy Roosevelt?

Materials
- 1 1¾oz/50g ball (each approx 104yd/95m) of Sirdar Ophelia (acrylic/nylon/polyester) each in #111 Perrie (A) and #067 Taupe (B) 〔4〕
- One pair size 9 (5.5mm) needles, **OR SIZE TO OBTAIN GAUGE**

- 2 small blue beads for eyes
- Purple ribbon 1½"/4cm wide
- Stitch markers
- Polyester stuffing
- Tapestry needle

Gauge

18 sts and 21 rows to 4"/10cm over seed st using size 9 (5.5mm) needles.
TAKE TIME TO CHECK GAUGE.

Seed Stitch

(over an odd number of sts)
Row 1 *K1, p1; rep from *, end k1.
Rep row 1 for seed st.

Square

(approx 10"/25.5cm square)
With A, cast on 45 sts. Work in seed st for 52 rows, or until piece is square.
Bind off.

Ears

With A, cast on 18 sts. Knit 2 rows.
Join B and knit 1 row.
*Pass 2nd st over first st and off the needle; rep from * until 1 st remains.
Secure last st. Weave in ends.

Tail

With A, cast on 5 sts. Work St st (k on RS, p on WS) for 1"/2.5cm.
Next row (RS) Ssk, k1, k2tog—3 sts.
Next row (WS) Slip 1, p2tog, psso.
Secure last st. Sew tail seam.

Tummy Piece (optional)

With B, cast on 11 sts.
Row 1 (RS) *K1, p1; rep from *, end k1.
Rows 2–5 Cast on 1 st, cont in seed st to the end—15 sts at end of row 5.
Rows 6–11 Work even in seed st.
Rows 12–19 K2tog, work seed st to end—7 sts at end of row 19.
Bind off.

. . . .

Assembly

Lay square on a flat surface.
Mark the center 23 sts along cast-on edge.
Mark center st, measure up 16 rows from center st and place another marker. Cut a piece of color A approx 25"/63.5cm long and sew running sts to outline the head, following the diagram for placement and leaving a long length at both ends.
Mark the center 15 sts along bound-off edge.

Cut a piece of color A approx 15"/38cm long and loop through these 15 sts, leaving a long length at both ends, for the butt.
Place markers along each side edge at 16 rows from cast-on and bound-off edges to mark each leg.

Head

Pull both ends of the running-st yarn that marked the head, gathering the fabric until the outer edges meet at the center, then tie the ends in a double knot tightly. Stuff the head firmly. Fold head in half, pin and sew cast-on sts tog for chin seam.

Front Legs

Fold one front leg so that side edges meet (blue dotted lines) and form a point at the outer edge (toe), easing the longer edge into the shorter edge and pin the edges together. Sew the side edges together. Fold and sew the other front leg in same way. Stuff the legs firmly.

Butt

Pull both ends of the yarn that marked the butt, gathering the fabric, then tie the ends in a double knot.
Be sure that the yarn is pulled tightly.

Back Legs

Fold one back leg so that side edges meet (green dotted lines) and form a point at the outer edge and pin the edges together. Sew the side edges together.
Fold and sew the other back leg in same way. Stuff the legs firmly.

Tummy

Stuff the remainder of the body tightly. Pin the remaining two sides together and with A, sew the tummy seam. Sew the tummy piece to tummy, following photo.

Finishing Details

Sew ears to head, leaving approx ¾"/24cm between the ears (use photo as a guide).
Sew on beads for eyes.
Sew tail to top of butt.
With B, embroider nose with satin st in center of face, then embroider mouth with straight sts.
Tie ribbon in a bow around the neck. ✿

Yin & Yang the Fighting Fish

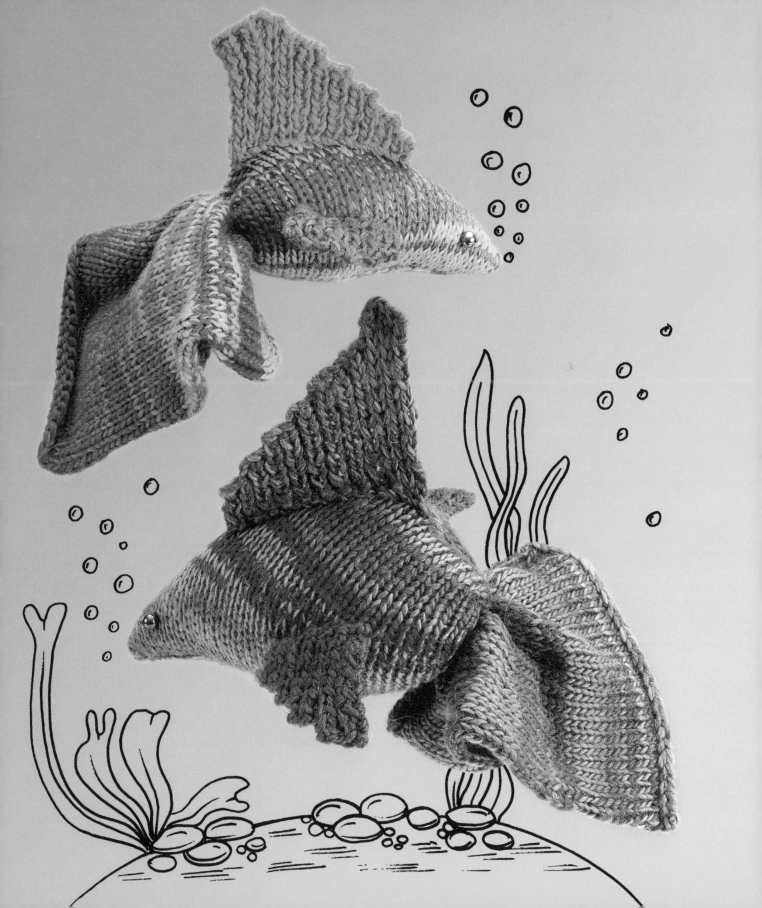

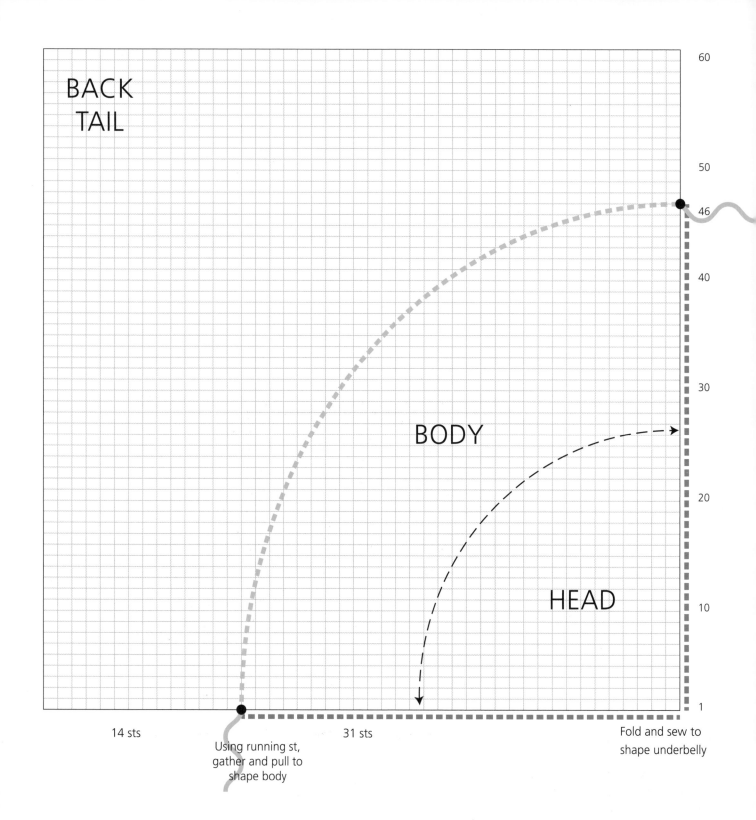

BACK
TAIL

BODY

HEAD

60

50

46

40

30

20

10

1

14 sts

31 sts

Fold and sew to
shape underbelly

Using running st,
gather and pull to
shape body

– – – = Fold line   ● = Marker

Yin & Yang often fight over who has the prettiest colors, but they always manage to remain friends.

Materials
- 1 1¾oz/50g balls (each approx 195yd/176m) of Crystal Palace Mini Mochi Plus (merino wool) in #555 Tapestry Rainbow or #553 Violet Rainbow (4)
- One pair size 8 (5mm) needles, OR SIZE TO OBTAIN GAUGE
- Two beads for eyes
- Stitch markers
- Polyester stuffing
- Tapestry needle

Gauge
18 sts and 24 rows to 4"/10cm over St st using size 8 (5mm) needles.
TAKE TIME TO CHECK GAUGE.

Square
(approx 10"/25.5cm square)
With desired color, cast on 45 sts. Work in St st (k on RS, p on WS) for 60 rows.
Bind off.

Small Fin (make 2)
Cast on 14 sts.
Row 1 (RS) *K1, p1; rep from * to end.
Rep row 1 for k1, p1 ribbing for 3 more rows.
Row 5 (RS) Bind off 3 sts, work in ribbing to end.
Row 6 Work even in ribbing.
Rows 7–10 Rep last 2 rows 2 more times. Bind off rem 5 sts.

Big Fin
Cast on 24 sts.
Row 1 (RS) *K1, p1; rep from * to end.
Rep row 1 for k1, p1 ribbing for 3 more rows.
Row 5 (RS) Bind off 3 sts, work in ribbing to end.
Row 6 Work even in ribbing.
Rows 7–12 Rep last 2 rows 3 more times.
Row 13 Bind off 6 sts, work in ribbing to end.
Row 14 Work even in ribbing.

Rows 15 and 16 Rep rows 13 and 14. Secure last st.

· ·

Assembly
Lay square on a flat surface.
Mark the 31st st along cast-on edge and 46th row and baste around square following yellow dotted lines on diagram, leaving a long length at both ends. Gather to shape the body and secure the ends.

Note if there is enough yarn, you can use these ends to sew the under belly.
Fold the cast-on sts and rows (along the red dotted lines) and sew together to shape the under belly, stuffing while sewing. The gathered fabric forms the back tail.

Finishing Details
Sew the big fin along the center back. Sew the small fins on either side of the big fin (see photo). Sew on beads for eyes. ✿

Freddy the Frog Prince

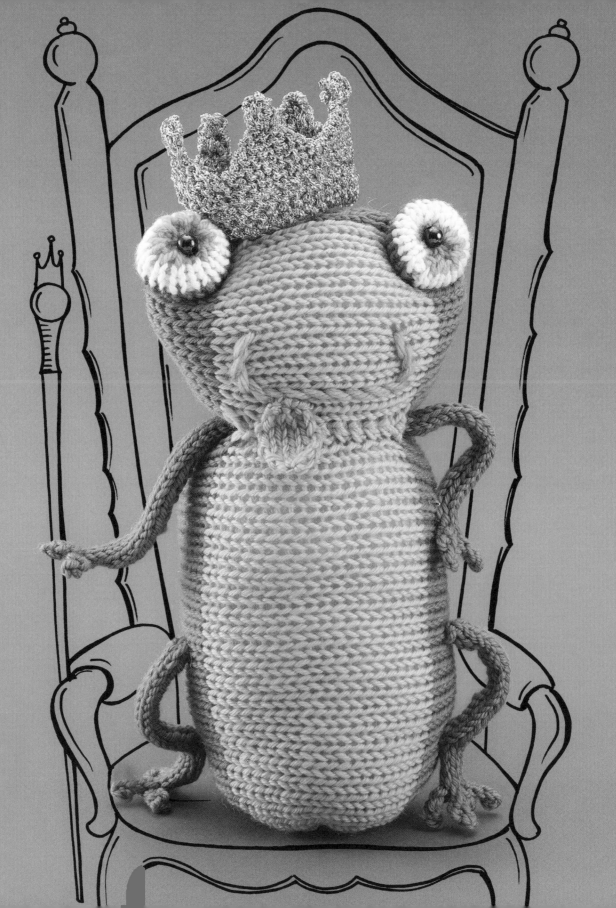

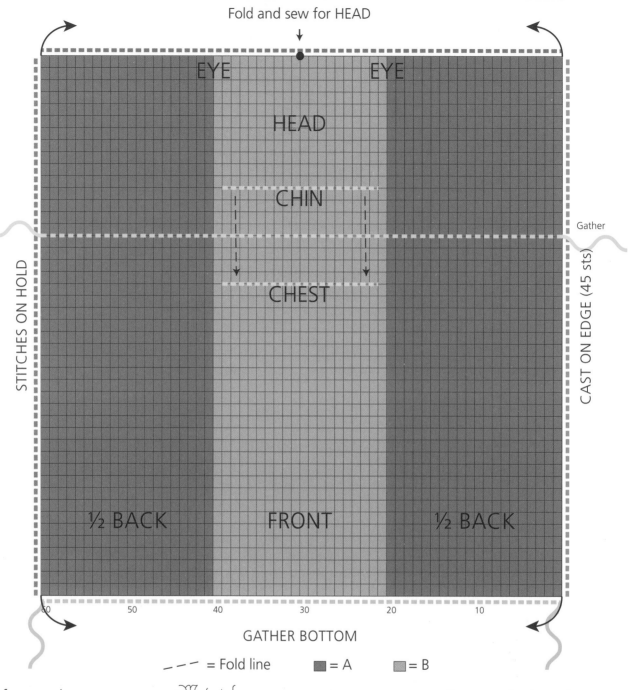

Fold and sew for HEAD ↓

EYE · EYE

HEAD

CHIN

CHEST

STITCHES ON HOLD

CAST ON EDGE (45 sts)

Gather

½ BACK · FRONT · ½ BACK

60 · 50 · 40 · 30 · 20 · 10

GATHER BOTTOM

– – – = Fold line   ■ = A   ■ = B

Kiss a frog and
you could get a prince...
or maybe
just frog breath!

Materials

- 1 3½oz/100g ball (each approx 220yd/200m) of Cascade 220 Superwash (superwash wool) each in #802 Green Apple (A) and #851 Lime Green (B) (4)
- Small amount in #877 Golden (C) and #871 White (D)
- 1 .88oz/25g ball (each approx 109yd/100m) of Rowan Anchor Artiste Metallic (viscose/metallized polyester) in #300 Gold (E) (1)
- Small amount of pink yarn for tongue and mouth
- One pair each sizes 5 and 7 (3.75 and 4.5mm) needles, OR SIZE TO OBTAIN GAUGE
- Two size 7 (4.5mm) double-pointed needles (dpn) for arms and legs only
- 2 beads for eyes
- Stitch markers
- Polyester stuffing
- Tapestry needle

Gauge

18 sts and 24 rows to 4"/10cm over St st using size 7 (4.5mm) needles and 220 Superwash.
TAKE TIME TO CHECK GAUGE

Provisional Cast-On

Note If you prefer not to use a provisional cast on, you can use a traditional cast-on. Using scrap yarn and crochet hook, chain the number of sts to cast on plus a few extra. Cut a tail and pull the tail through the last chain. With knitting needle and yarn, pick up and knit the stated number of sts through the "purl bumps" on the back of the chain. To remove scrap yarn chain, when instructed, pull out the tail from the last crochet stitch. Gently and slowly pull on the tail to unravel the crochet stitches, carefully placing each released knit stitch on a needle.

Square

(approx 10"/25.5cm square)
With size 7 (4.5mm) needles and A, cast on 45 sts using provisional cast on.
Rows 1–20 With A, work in St st (k on RS, p on WS). Cut A, join B.
Rows 21–40 With B, work in St st. Cut B, join A.
Rows 41–60 With A, work in St st. Do *not* bind off. Leave sts on needle. (If using traditional cast on, bind off the sts.)

Eyes (make 2)

With size 7 (4.5mm) needles and C, cast on 8 sts.
Row 1 (RS) Kfb in every st—16 sts.
Rows 2–4 With D, purl 1 row, knit 1 row, purl 1 row.
Rows 5–8 With A, cont in St st.
Row 9 (RS) K1, *k2tog; rep from * to last st, k1—9 sts.
Row 10 *P2tog; rep from *, end k1—5 sts. Pass all sts over the first and off the needle one at a time. Secure last st. Stuff eyes and sew seams.

Arms (make 2)

With dpn and A, cast on 5 sts.
Work I-cord as foll:

*Row 1 (RS)** Knit. Do *not* turn work. Slide the sts back to the opposite end of needle to work next row from RS. Pull yarn tightly from the end of the row. Rep from * for 24 rows. Without turning work, slide the sts back to the opposite end of needle to work next row from RS. Using cable cast on, cast on 4 sts, bind off 4 sts, k1, [cast on 4 sts, bind off 4 sts] twice, k1—5 sts. Pass all sts over the first and off the needle one at a time. Secure last st.

Legs (make 2)

Work same as arms.

Tongue

With size 7 (4.5mm) needles and pink yarn, cast on 5 sts.
Beg with a knit row, work in St st for 4 rows.
Row 5 (RS) Ssk, k1, k2tog—3 sts.
Row 6 Sl 1, p2tog, psso. Secure last st.

Crown

With size 5 (3.75mm) needles and 2 strands E held tog, cast on 6 sts.
Row 1 (RS) K3, yo, k3—7 sts.
Row 2 and all WS rows through row 10 Knit.
Row 3 K3, yo, k4—8 sts.
Row 5 K3, yo, k5—9 sts.
Row 7 K3, yo, k6—10 sts.
Row 9 K3, yo, k7—11 sts.
Row 11 K3, yo, k7, make bobble as foll: (k1, p1) twice into final st—4 sts, [turn, sl 1, k3] 4 times, turn, lift all sts over the first st and off the needle one at a time—12 sts.
Row 12 Bind off 6 sts, k to end—6 sts.
Rep rows 1–12 four more times.
Bind off. Sew cast-on and bound-off edges tog.

· ·

Assembly

Using Kitchener stitch, join cast-on edge to sts on needle (if using a regular cast on, sew edges tog).

Bottom

With tapestry needle and long length of A, loop all sts on one edge, pull tightly, secure for bottom (see orange dotted line on schematic). Stuff ¾ of the way.

Head

Along opposite edge from bottom, count down 15 sts on each side, run gathering st around tube (yellow dotted line), pull to shape neck (see photo).
Stuff head, pin back to front top opening and sew straight across (purple dotted line).
Fold chin to chest (pink dotted lines) and sew sts from chin and chest tog.
With C, sew eyes onto each side of head from front to back and tie tightly.
This flattens the eyes shapes the head of the frog.
Sew bead in center of each eye.
Sew arms and legs in place (see photo).
Sew crown to center top of frogs head.

Finishing Details

With pink yarn, embroider mouth with stem stitch. Sew on tongue under mouth (see photo for placement). ✿

Sampson the Sheep Dog

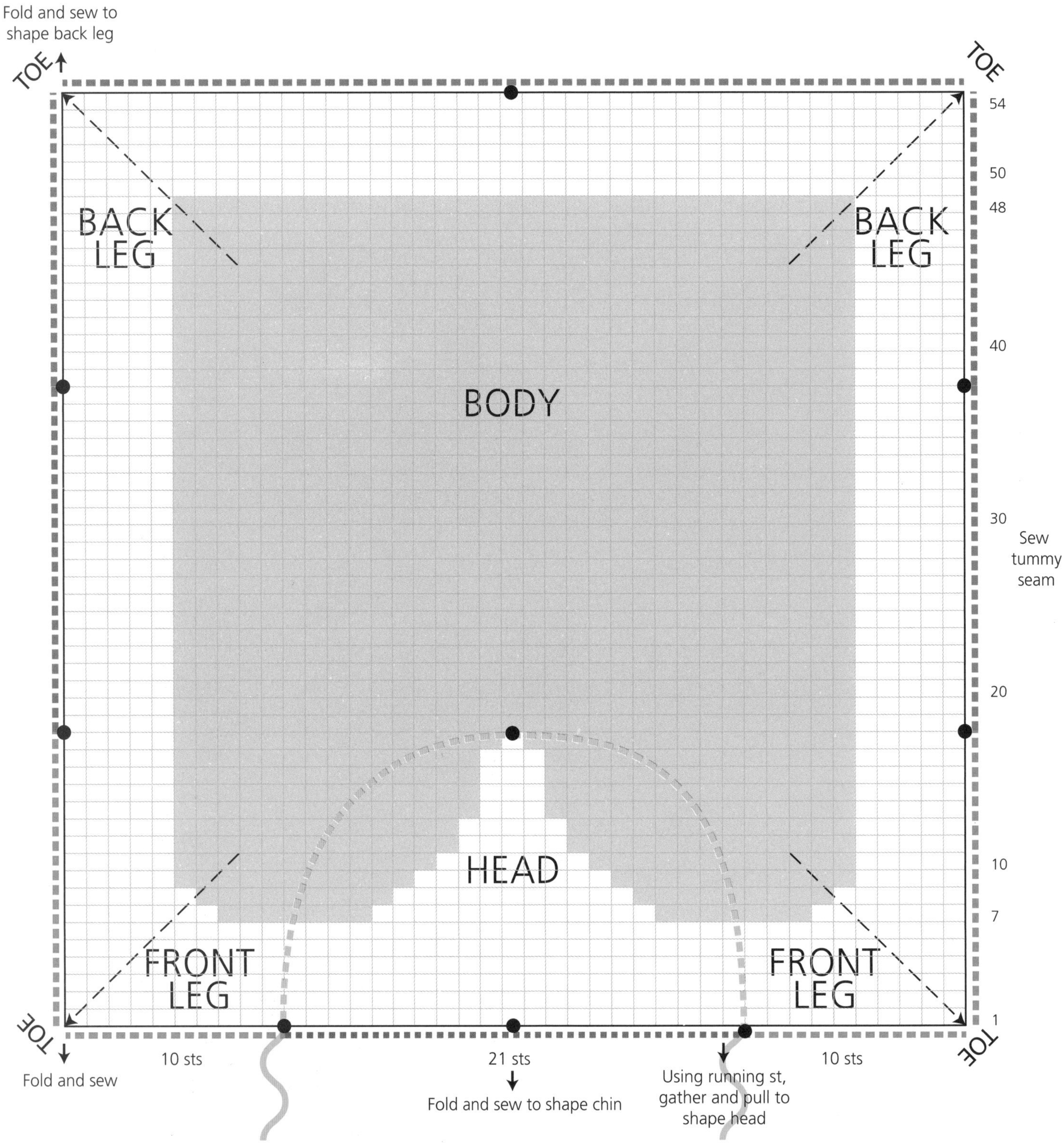

Fold and sew to
shape back leg

TOE ↑

TOE

BACK
LEG

BACK
LEG

54

50

48

●

●

40

BODY

30

Sew
tummy
seam

20

●

●

HEAD

10

7

FRONT
LEG

FRONT
LEG

TOE ↓

1

Fold and sew

10 sts

21 sts

10 sts

Fold and sew to shape chin

Using running st,
gather and pull to
shape head

– – – = Fold line   ● = Marker

□ = A   ▨ = B

134

Sampson keeps
a keen eye over all the
sheep. He knows
we want more wool!

Materials
- 1 3/4oz/50g skein (each approx 27yd/25m) of Lion Brand Yarn Romance (nylon/polyester) each in #100 Silky White (A) and #149 Grey Shades (B) (6)
- One pair size 7 (4.5mm) needles, OR SIZE TO OBTAIN GAUGE
- Two size 7 (4.5mm) double-pointed needles (dpn)
- Small amount of pink yarn for tongue and black yarn for nose
- 2 black beads for eyes, corresponding yarn for sewing
- Stitch markers
- Polyester stuffing
- Tapestry needle

Gauge
18 sts and 24 rows to 4"/10cm over St st using size 7 (4.5mm) needles.
TAKE TIME TO CHECK GAUGE

Notes
1) Fur yarn must be used to get the sheep dog look. Fur yarn can be tricky to knit. Count your sts every row.
2) The chart is worked in St st but the RS of the fabric will be the purl side, which shows the fluffiness of the yarn better.
3) When working chart, use separate lengths (butterflies) of yarn for each block of color and when changing colors, twist yarns on WS to prevent holes in work.

Square
(approx 9"/23cm square)
With A, cast on 41 sts. Working in St st follow chart for 54 rows. Bind off.

Ears
With A, cast on 6 sts. Knit 1 row. Bind off.

Tail
With A, cast on 7 sts. Knit 1 row. Bind off.

Tongue
With pink, cast on 5 sts. Bind off 5 sts.

. . . .

Assembly
Lay square on a flat surface.
Mark the center 21 sts along cast-on edge. Mark center st, measure up 17 rows from center st and place another marker. Cut a piece of yarn approx 25"/63.5cm long and sew running sts to outline the head, following the diagram for placement and leaving a long length at both ends.
Place markers along each side edge at 17 rows from cast-on and bound-off edges to mark one half of each leg.
Mark the center st along bound-off edge to mark other half of each back leg.

Head
Pull both ends of the running-st yarn that marked the head, gathering the fabric until the outer edges meet at the center, then tie the ends in a double knot tightly. Stuff the head firmly. Fold head in half, pin and sew cast-on sts tog for chin seam.

Front Legs
Fold one front leg so that side edges (blue dotted lines) meet and form a point at the outer edge (toe), easing the longer side into the shorter side, and pin the edges together. Sew the side edges together. Fold and sew the other front leg in same way. Stuff the legs firmly.

Back Legs
Fold one back leg so that side edges (green dotted lines) meet at the center marked st and form a point at the outer edge (toe) easing the longer side into the shorter side, and pin the edges together. Sew the side edges together.
Fold and sew the other back leg in same way. Stuff the legs firmly.

Tummy
Stuff the remainder of the body firmly. Pin the remaining two sides together and sew the tummy seam.

Finishing Details
Sew ears to head, leaving approx 1½"/4cm between the ears.
Sew tail to top of butt.
Sew on beads for eyes.
With black yarn, embroider satin st for nose.
Sew tongue under nose. ✿

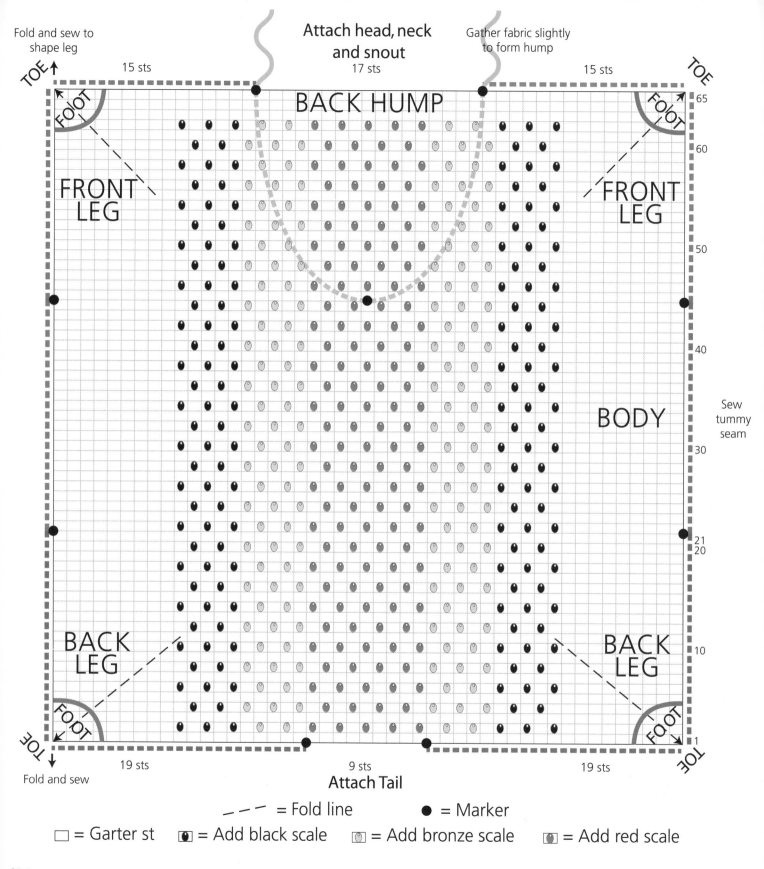

Fold and sew to shape leg

Attach head, neck and snout

Gather fabric slightly to form hump

TOE↑

15 sts

17 sts

15 sts

TOE

FOOT

BACK HUMP

65

FOOT

FRONT LEG

FRONT LEG

60

50

40

BODY

Sew tummy seam

30

21
20

10

BACK LEG

BACK LEG

FOOT

FOOT

TOE↓

1

19 sts

9 sts

19 sts

TOE

Fold and sew

Attach Tail

- - - = Fold line   ● = Marker

□ = Garter st   🖤 = Add black scale   🤍 = Add bronze scale   🖤 = Add red scale

Drake's fiery breath
can defend any castle, but
knitting him up is
one cool experience.

Materials
- 1 3½oz/100g hank (each approx 210yd/190m) of Sudio Donegal Soft Donegal from Leilani Arts (merino wool) in #5208 Oatmeal (4)
- Small amount of black yarn for claws and embroidery
- Small amount of gold metallic yarn for fire
- One pair size 7 (4.5mm) needles, OR SIZE TO OBTAIN GAUGE
- 2 Steampunk Charms, Steam 178 (dragon eyes, bright) from solidoakonline.com
- Dragon Scales from colettesgarden.com in red, black and bronze
- Stitch markers
- Polyester stuffing
- Tapestry needle

Gauge
20 sts and 26 rows to 4"/10cm over St st using size 7 (4.5mm) needles.
TAKE TIME TO CHECK GAUGE

Attach a Scale
Note Adding 1 scale takes 2 sts.
On a WS row, insert RH needle into first st as if to knit. Slip scale onto RH needle through the scale hole, curved side facing outward. Loop yarn around RH needle, above scale, and draw the yarn through the scale hole, then through the stitch, and off the LH needle. Knit the 2nd st, securing the scale in place.

Square
(approx 10"/25.5cm square)

Cast on 47 sts. Work in garter st (knit every row), adding scales as shown on diagram (note that even rows of chart are WS rows), through row 65. Bind off.

Neck and Snout
Cast on 17 sts and follow chart for neck (page 140) in garter stitch through row 22. Knit 3 rows, ending with a RS row.
Cont, shaping snout as foll:
Row 1 (WS) P2tog, p to last 2 sts, p2tog—15 sts.
Rows 2 and 4 Knit.
Row 3 Purl.
Row 5 (WS) Rep row 1—13 sts.
Row 6 Knit.
Rep last 2 rows until 7 sts rem.
Knit 1 row. Bind off.

Tail
Cast on 3 sts.
Knit 3 rows.
Beg chart for tail (page 140) as foll:
Row 1 (RS) Knit.
Row 2 (WS) K1, add red scale, k1.
Row 3 Kfb, k to last st, kfb—2 sts inc'd.
Row 4 [K1, add red scale] 2 times, k1.
Cont to work chart in this way (there are 15 sts after working row 23) through row 53. Bind off.

Left Wing
Cast on 7 sts, leaving a long tail for sewing.
Row 1 (RS) K1, *p1, k1; rep from * to end.
Row 2 P1, *k1, p1; rep from * to end.
Row 3 K1, *p1, M1p, k1; rep from * to end—10 sts.
Row 4 P1, *k2, p1; rep from * to end.
Row 5 K1, *p2, M1p, k1; rep from * to end—13 sts.
Row 6 P1, *k3, p1; rep from * to end
Row 7 K1, *p3, M1p, k1; rep from * to end—16 sts.
Row 8 P1, *k4, p1; rep from * to end.
Row 9 K1, *p4, M1p, k1; rep from * to end—19 sts.
Row 10 P1, *k5, p1; rep from * to end.
Rows 11 and 13 K1, *p5, k1; rep from * to end.
Rows 12 and 14 P1, *k5, p1; rep from * to end.
Row 15 Bind off 6 sts, cont in pat as established to end—13 sts.
Rows 16–18 Cont in pat as established.
Row 19 Rep row 15—7 sts.
Rows 20–22 Cont in pat as established. Bind off.

Right Wing
Work same as left wing through row 13.
Row 14 (WS) Bind off 6 sts, cont in pat as established to end—13 sts.
Rows 15–17 Cont in pat as established.
Row 18 Rep row 14—7 sts.
Rows 19–21 Cont in pat as established. Bind off.

Eyelids (make 2)
Cast on 5 sts.
Row 1 (RS) Kfb, k to last st, kfb—7sts.
Row 2 Purl.
Bind off, leaving a tail for attaching.

Claws (make 4)
Using a single cast on, with black yarn, *cast on 6 sts, bind off 5 sts. Place rem st on LH needle.
Rep from * two more times. Secure last st.

. . . .

Assembly
Lay square on a flat surface.
Mark the center 17 along bound-off edge. Count down 21 rows from center st and place marker. Cut a piece of yarn approx 25"/63.5cm long and sew running sts to outline the back hump, following the diagram for placement and leaving a long length at both ends. Mark the center 9 along cast-on edge for tail. Place markers along each side edge at 21 rows from cast-on and bound-off edges to mark one half of each leg.

Hump

Sew cast-on edge of neck to center 17 sts of bound-off edge of square. Pull both ends of the running-st yarn that marked the hump,
gathering the fabric to form the front hump, then tie the ends in a double knot tightly. Stuff the hump, neck, head and snout firmly, sewing the neck and snout seam while stuffing.

Front Legs

Fold one front leg so that side edges (blue dotted lines) meet and form a point at the outer edge (toe), easing the longer side into the shorter side, and pin the edges together. Sew the side edges together. Fold and sew the other front leg in same way. Stuff the legs firmly.

Back Legs

Fold one back leg so that side edges (green dotted lines) meet and form a point at the outer edge (toe), easing the longer side into the shorter side, and pin the edges together. Sew the side edges together. Fold and sew the other back leg in same way. Stuff the legs firmly.

Tail and Tummy

Sew tail seam, stuffing as you sew. Sew tail to center 9 sts of cast-on edge of square. Stuff the remainder of the body firmly. Pin the remaining two sides together and sew the tummy seam.

Finishing Details

Wrap a length of black yarn around tip of leg (red line on diagram) to create foot, then attach a claw to front of toe. Repeat for each leg. Sew wings to top of front.
Sew cast-on edge of eyelids where snout shaping begins, letting bound-off edge curl to the front. Sew beads for eyes under eyelids. With black yarn, embroider two French knots for nostrils. Attach short lengths of metallic yarn to tip of snout for fire (see photo). ❀

TAIL CHART

15 sts

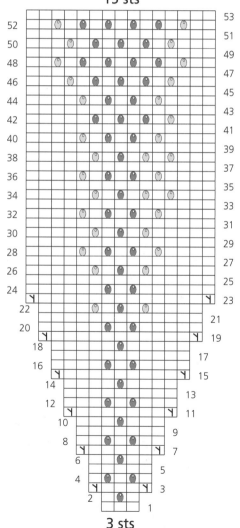

NECK CHART

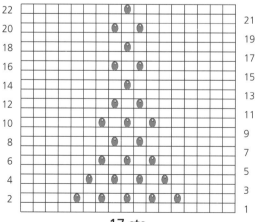

3 sts

17 sts

KEY

☐ = Garter st

丫 = Kfb

⬮ = Add bronze scale

⬮ = Add red scale

Acknowledgments

Many thanks to the following amazing people for their invaluable contributions to making this book beautiful and fun.

Sixth&Spring Books — Great support, as always, from Trisha Malcolm, Art Joinnides, Jay Stein, Joan Krellenstein, and Carrie Kilmer.

Keely Brandon — Special thanks for her artistic talent and descriptive illustrations, which provided such innovative and whimsical backgrounds for the animals.

Joe Vior — Master art director and visionary, for his inspired and tireless work that gave all my animals their beautiful environments.

Diane Lamphron — For her initial artistic input.

Jack Deutsch — For his incredible photography and mastery, which gave inanimate objects such vibrant life. Thanks also to his hardworking assistants Stephen Reganato and Keith Greenbaum.

Carla Scott — My friend and amazing instruction writer.

Jacob Seifert — For his diligence in keeping track of all the animals and making sure everything in the book was complete and perfect.

Matthew Schrank — For his efficient ordering of all the yarns for the book.

Loretta Dachman — A big thank-you for the hours that went into creating the beautiful, clear charts.

Heris Stenzel — For her wonderful typing and always being there for me.

My team of friends and fantastic knitters who help make my dreams come true — Jo Brandon, Emily Brenner, Eileen Curry, Phyllis Ross, Dianne Weitzul, and Nancy Henderson.

My personal pals, supporters and animal lovers — Christine Farrow, Dana Quinones, Mary Spagnuolo, Barbara Spohn, Jim Spohn, Roxanne Hunt, Marla Falco, Marilyn Tomlinson, Jennifer Wilson, Hugh Jackman, Betty Hagi, Debbie Macomber, Roberta Stalberg, and Leigh Merrifield.

Thank you to all the generous yarn companies (please see page 144 for complete list).

And thanks to all the children, big and small, who inspired me to do this book and who show all animals, whether they are real or stuffed, unconditional love.

Things to Know

SINGLE CAST-ON

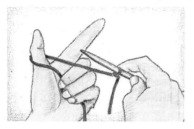

1. Place a slipknot on the right needle, leaving a short tail. Wrap the yarn from the ball around your left thumb from front to back and secure it in your palm with your other fingers.

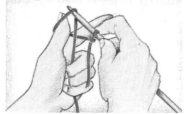

2. Insert the needle upward through the strand on your thumb.

3. Slip this loop from your thumb onto the needle, pulling the yarn from the ball to tighten it. Continue in this way until all the stitches are cast on.

EMBROIDERY STITCHES

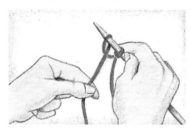

LAZY DAISY STITCH

RUNNING STITCH

STRAIGHT STITCH

FRENCH KNOT

STEM STITCH

DUPLICATE STITCH

SATIN STITCH

ABBREVIATIONS

approx	approximately
beg	begin(ning)
CC	contrasting color
cm	centimeter(s)
cn	cable needle
cont	continu(e)(ing)
dec	decreas(e)(ing)
dpn	double-pointed needle(s)
foll	follow(s)(ing)
g	gram(s)
inc	increas(e)(ing)
k	knit
kfb	knit into front and back of stitch
k2tog	knit 2 stitches together
LH	left-hand
lp(s)	loop(s)
m	meter(s)
MC	main color
mm	millimeter(s)
M1(p)	make one (purl): with needle tip, lift strand between last stitch knit (purled) and the next stitch on the LH needle and knit (purl) into back of it
oz	ounce(s)
p	purl
pat(s)	pattern(s)
psso	pass slip stitch(es) over
p2tog	purl 2 stitches together
rem	remain(s)(ing)
rep	repeat
rev St st	reverse stockinette st: purl on RS, k on WS
RH	right-hand
rnd(s)	round(s)
RS	right side(s)
SKP	slip 1, knit 1, pass slip st over
SK2P	slip 1, k2tog, pass sl st over the k2 together
sl	slip
sl st	slip stitch
ssk	slip 2 sts tog knitwise, insert left-hand needle into fronts of these stitches and knit them together
st(s)	stitch(es)
St st	stockinette stitch: k on RS, p on WS
tbl	through back loop(s)
tog	together
WS	wrong side(s)
wyib	with yarn in back
wyif	with yarn in front
yd	yard(s)
yo	yarn over needle
*	repeat directions following * as many times as indicated
[ ]	repeat directions inside brackets as many times as indicated

1) Hold the end of the yarn with your thumb. Bring the yarn around your forefinger and middle finger. Wrap it in the opposite direction around your ring and little finger. Continue wrapping the yarn in a figure eight until you have the desired amount of yarn.

2) Cut the yarn, leaving about an 8"/20cm tail. Remove the yarn from your fingers, wrap the tail several times around the center and tie a knot as shown. Pull the unknotted end of the strand to release the yarn as needed.

I-CORD

Cast on about three to five stitches. *Knit one row. Without turning the work, slip the stitches back to the beginning of the row. Pull the yarn tightly from the end of the row. Repeat from * until desired length. Bind off.

Standard Yarn Weight System

Categories of yarn, gauge ranges, and recommended needle and hook sizes

Yarn Weight Symbol & Category	🧶0 Lace	🧶1 Super Fine	🧶2 Fine	🧶3 Light	🧶4 Medium	🧶5 Bulky	🧶6 Super Bulky	🧶7 Jumbo
Type of Yarns in Category	Fingering 10-count crochet thread	Sock, Fingering, Baby	Sport, Baby	DK, Light Worsted	Worsted, Afghan, Aran	Chunky, Craft, Rug	Super Bulky, Roving	Jumbo, Roving
Knit Gauge Range* in Stockinette Stitch to 4 inches	33–40** sts	27–32 sts	23–26 sts	21–24 sts	16–20 sts	12–15 sts	7–11 sts	6 sts and fewer
Recommended Needle in Metric Size Range	1.5–2.25 mm	2.25—3.25 mm	3.25—3.75 mm	3.75—4.5 mm	4.5—5.5 mm	5.5—8 mm	8—12.75 mm	12.75 mm and larger
Recommended Needle U.S. Size Range	000–1	1 to 3	3 to 5	5 to 7	7 to 9	9 to 11	11 to 17	17 and larger
Crochet Gauge* Ranges in Single Crochet to 4 inch	32–42 double crochets**	21–32 sts	16–20 sts	12–17 sts	11–14 sts	8–11 sts	6–9 sts	5 sts and fewer
Recommended Hook in Metric Size Range	Steel*** 1.6–1.4 mm	2.25—3.5 mm	3.5—4.5 mm	4.5—5.5 mm	5.5—6.5 mm	6.5—9 mm	9—16 mm	16 mm and larger
Recommended Hook U.S. Size Range	Steel*** 6, 7, 8 Regular hook B-1	B-1 to E-4	E-4 to 7	7 to I-9	I-9 to K-10 1/2	K-10 1/2 to M-13	M-13 to Q	Q and larger

* GUIDELINES ONLY: The above reflect the most commonly used gauges and needle or hook sizes for specific yarn categories.

** Lace weight yarns are usually knitted or crocheted on larger needles and hooks to create lacy, openwork patterns. Accordingly, a gauge range is difficult to determine. Always follow the gauge stated in your pattern.

*** Steel crochet hooks are sized differently from regular hooks—the higher the number, the smaller the hook, which is the reverse of regular hook sizing

This Standards & Guidelines booklet and downloadable symbol artwork are available at: **YarnStandards.com**

GAUGE

Make a test swatch at least 4"/10cm square. If the number of stitches and rows does not correspond to the gauge given, you must change the needle size. An easy rule to follow is: To get fewer stitches to the inch/cm, use a larger needle; to get more stitches to the inch/cm, use a smaller needle. Continue to try different needle sizes until you get the same number of stitches in the gauge.

Index & Resources

The BagSmith
www.bagsmith.com

Berroco
www.berroco.com

Cascade Yarns
www.cascadeyarns.com

Colette's Garden
www.colettesgarden.com

Crystal Palace Yarns
www.straw.com

**Filatura di Crosa/
Tahki•Stacy Charles**
www.tahkistacycharles.com

Koigu
www.koigu.com/yarns.html

Leilani Arts
www.leilaniarts.net

Lion Brand Yarn
www.lionbrand.com

Madelinetosh
www.madelinetosh.com

Noro/KFI
www.knittingfever.com

Premier Yarns
www.premieryarns.com

Plymouth Yarn
www.plymouthyarn.com

Rowan
www.knitrowan.com

Sirdar
www.sirdar.co.uk

Solid Oak
www.solidoakonline.com

Studio Donegal
www.studiodonegal.ie